Papercraft

Papercraft

Over 15 step-by-step projects to make and give

Emma Angel

C&B

Disclaimer

The lamp shade used on the cover is not recommended for use with candles.

The author and publishers have made every effort to ensure that all instructions in this book are accurate and safe. They cannot accept any liability for injury, damage, or loss to persons, however it may arise.

Photo Credits

The publisher wishes to thank Simon Clay for taking all the photography in this book, including the images on the front and back covers.
All photography is copyright © PRC Publishing.
All enquiries regarding the images should be referred to Chrysalis Images.

Acknowledgments

A big "thank you" to the following people:
Ella Chegwyn, Louise McSweeney, and Debbie Webb for allowing their designs to be shown in this book.
Thanks to my boyfriend Jon for all the love and for cooking for me while I have been writing this book. Thanks to my mum Katherine for the inspiration. Thanks to my chums Lucy Clink and Emily Ward, for being my chums.

Thank you to:
Rubinato for the beautiful inks, pens, and seals
Kate at The Papershed for her help and papermaking supplies.
Roz at Creative Crafts for her advice.
Sarah Glennie at GFSmith and Caroline Bartl at Funky Eclectica.
And thank you to Kate at PRC for her amazing organizational skills.

For more information on contributors to this book, visit
www.emmaangel.co.uk

Produced 2003 by
PRC Publishing Ltd,
64 Brewery Road, London N7 9NT
A member of **Chrysalis** Books plc

First published in Great Britain in 2003 by
Collins & Brown
64 Brewery Road
London N7 9NT
A member of **Chrysalis** Books plc

1 2 3 4 5 6 7 8 9

ISBN: 1-84340-117-7

Printed in Malaysia

Contents

Papercrafting: An Introduction 6

Part One: Getting Started

Equipment 8, Safety 10, Basic Papermaking 11, Papermaking 14,
Texturing, Casting, Molding, and Waterproofing 16,
Choosing Paper and Card 18,
Equipment Needed 20, Embellishments 21

Part Two: Crafting

Personal Events

A New Home 22
Baby 26
Wedding 30
Bon Voyage Book 34
Anniversary 38
Get Well Soon 42

Birthdays

Birthday Boy 46
Birthday Girl 50
Teens 54
Grandparents 58

Just to Say . . .

Hello 62
Thank You 66
Sorry 70

Holidays

Valentine's Day 74
Easter 78
Mother's Day 82
Halloween 86
Winter Holidays 90
Angel Decorations 94

Templates 96

Papercrafting: An Introduction

Papermaking is not an expensive hobby, especially if you use recycled paper and turn old stock into attractive new sheets. This book is divided into two sections: the first tells you how to make your own gorgeously unique handmade paper, and the second shows you how to craft it.

Handmade paper

While making handmade paper, you can also learn how to color it, using dye, paint, wax, and splash effects. You may also want to embed the pieces you have made with treasures such as silk strands and petals, or even scent them. As well as making your own pieces, you could also choose from the wide variety of papers that are available from around the world—the "Choosing paper and card" section gives advice on what is available.

Cards and gifts

In Part 2, "Crafting," there are nineteen innovative paper projects showing you how to make greeting cards and keepsakes for friends and family. You can learn how to make cards for birthdays and weddings or for those important dates in your diary, such as Valentine's Day and Christmas. Putting thought and attention into making gifts shows just how much you care, and there are ideas for adapting each of the gift projects to capture something of the personalities of the giver and receiver. There are lots of different techniques and papers for you to experiment with and enjoy, and the final project encompasses all the techniques learned to create contemporary Christmas decorations.

What is paper made of?

From paper cups, plates, paperback books, money, dolls, bags, fans, shades, and hats to papier-mâché, wrapping paper, wallpaper, and newspapers, paper is everywhere! There's just no getting away from it, as it's so incredibly versatile. It can be used to record and communicate ideas; for practical purposes in the form of boxes, cartons, and packaging to protect, store, and transport goods; or even just for decorative and artistic purposes.

But what is paper? Modern day paper can be described as thin sheets of pulped fibers. The pulp is made from beating fibers from wood, cotton, or hemp. The fibers then need to be put into water, allowing them to separate and float. A sieve or mesh strains the mixture and what is left on the mesh dries to form paper.

The origins of paper
Papyrus

Early civilizations used anything from cave walls, leaves, and bark, to animal skins, stone, and metal to write or draw on. It wasn't until about 4,000 B.C. that the Egyptians came up with an ingenious material to write on, when they figured out how to fashion a mat from the papyrus that grew around the banks of the Nile. Thin strips of the core of the plant were cut lengthwise and then laid out in two layers, horizontally and vertically on a smooth drying board. The strips were soaked in water and then pounded together. As they were drying, the gluey sap of the plant acted as an adhesive and stuck the layers together. The dried papyrus could be written on and rolled into scrolls for storing. Paper gets its name from "papyrus," although this is something of a misnomer, as the paper we know today is made from pulped wood fibers.

Pulp and Paper

In the first century A.D. Chinese artists and calligraphers painted and wrote on silk, but this was a very expensive and time-consuming material to make. Ts'ai Lun, a Chinese monk, was commissioned to come up with an alternative. He "pulped up" mulberry bark, hemp, and rags, pressed the pulp together and squeezed out the water. The result was then hung from a tree to dry in the sun. This humble start became one of humanity's greatest inventions, as revolutionary as the Internet is today. Modern paper evolved out of Ts'ai Lun's invention, but it wasn't until the end of the seventeenth century that it was made from wood pulp. The material we use today is made from wood fibers, but the basic principle for paper-making has changed little in two thousand years.

Part One: Getting Started

Equipment needed for making paper

There are two main processes in papermaking: beating materials to make pulp and forming the pulp into sheets. Commercial paper mills spray fibers onto fast-moving felt belts. However, you don't need such high-tech machines to make handmade paper. You can make your own paper mill at home from kitchen equipment and a few special items.

To beat your materials into a pulp, you can use a conventional handheld blender or food processor. However, use an old one that you won't need to use to prepare food.

Next, you will need a "mold and deckle" or two wooden frames of the same size that are used to form the sheets of paper. The mold and deckle can either be bought from a craft shop or made at home (see below) by stapling mesh over a frame. The mesh allows water to drain away, leaving only the fibers. The deckle frame is left empty and sits on top of the mesh to trap watery pulp. This is where the distinctive, uneven deckled edges on handmade paper come from. The deckle determines the size of the paper but not the thickness.

To make a "mold and deckle" you will need:

Strips of wood: four pieces 8 in. long and four pieces 13 in. long
Wood glue
Screws or nails and a screwdriver
 or hammer
Material for the mesh: Use a brass screen
 from a hardware shop or silk-screen
 mesh from an art shop
Staples and staple gun
A helper

1 Use wood glue to assemble two frames. When the frames have stuck together, screw them or nail them along the outside edge to secure them.

2 When the frames are finished, cover one of them with mesh, pulled as taut as possible (this is the mold) and leave the other empty (this is the deckle). The mesh needs to be larger than the interior of the frame by 2 in. Cut the mesh to size, and if using silk-screen fabric, wet it before stretching it.

3 Use a staple gun to attach the mesh—ask a helper to pull it taught as you staple around. In time the mesh may sag and need to be replaced by removing the old mesh and restapling.

As a quick improvisation, buy two picture frames of the same size. Staple silk-screen fabric to one of them to make the mold and leave the second frame bare to act as the deckle.

Equipment needed for making paper:

A vat: use a deep plastic toy box
Rubber gloves
Mold and deckle (see opposite)
Sieve
Bucket
Glass bowls
Airtight jars for storing left
  over pulp
Measuring jug and
  measuring spoons
Sponge
Pump action spray
  bottle
Brushes
Old toothbrush
Dropper

Equipment for drying:

Drying boards made of smooth plastic or wooden chopping boards can be used to ensure that one side of the paper is smooth. This makes it possible to rubber-stamp handmade paper. Alternatively, for a textured effect, use felt or a cloths such as a dish towel.

You will also need a hand towel for blotting the surface of the paper (an old, well-washed one is better than a new one that may leave fuzz behind).

Large hardback books can be used as weights or as a press.

Safety

Papercrafting is one of the safest crafts; however, there are always some points to bear in mind for any craft. Here are some potential hazards.

Adhesives and glues: Use nontoxic glues wherever possible. If you need to use stronger glue, keep it away from your skin.

Bleach (hydrogen peroxide): Used for lightening pulp. Can burn eyes and skin so it is advisable to wear rubber gloves and eye goggles when handling it. Work in a well-ventilated area and use respiratory protection. Protect your work surface and your clothing. Certain bleaching agents are harmful to the environment and should therefore be avoided or used sparingly.

Colorants: Some commercial dyes are toxic. Read manufacturers instructions, wear rubber gloves, and work in a well-ventilated area wearing a face mask.

Cutting equipment: Scissors and knives should be handled with care. If using a knife, put down a rubber cutting mat first, to protect the surface underneath. Always cut away from yourself.

Electrical safety: Making paper is a wet job. Mop up any spilled water and make sure hands are dry before touching anything electrical to avoid a shock.

Food processor: Keep equipment used for papercrafting separate from equipment used to prepare food.

Gloves and goggles: Wear rubber gloves and goggles when handling any chemicals.

Heat: Heat is needed to activate embossing powders—use either an old toaster or a special heat tool. Hold paper by the corners and keep hands away from direct heat to avoid burns.

Microwave: Used to melt candles for waxing paper. Use a microwaveable dish and heat-proof gloves when handling the hot dish.

Mordants: Needed to lock in colors. Most dyes come with their own mordants mixed in. If they are separate, read manufacturer's instructions before using.

Storage: Airtight jars can be used to store leftover pulp. The pulp needs to be kept cool in a refrigerator. Make sure jars are labeled clearly when stored in this way.

Straining: It is a good idea to strain any leftover pulp through a sieve before emptying the water down a drain. This will prevent any blockages from occurring.

Basic Papermaking

To start with, you need something to make a pulp from. You can recycle, use raw plants (garden plants and vegetables), or purchase paper crumbles (prebeaten fibers) from specialized suppliers. Paper crumbles (made from cotton, hemp, and wood fibers) are already broken up and will need to be soaked for half an hour or so.

Making paper from plants takes more time, as fibers need to be soaked and boiled before they can be beaten. However, recycling paper is a good way to learn the basics.

Recycling

Scraps left over from craft projects can be reused, as well as writing paper, computer papers, colored papers, photocopies, old envelopes, paper from used notebooks, magazines, flyers, and newspapers. Ask a printer or copy store for wastepaper or collect your own from the office or from most people's abundant supply of junk mail.

The type of paper used as stock will have a big effect on the resulting color. Newspaper will produce a mottled dark gray paper. Scrap colored papers mixed together will create new colors. For example, yellow and orange paper mixed together will create a yellowy orange finished paper. Wet pulp always looks darker, and once it has dried it will be a lighter by a couple of shades.

You can use white paper that has been printed on with black ink to produce a pale silver-gray paper or bleach the ink out of the paper to take it back to white. However, take care, as certain bleaching agents are harmful to the environment.

Preparing pulp

If you want to experiment with colorants, you will need a light-colored pulp to work with. Either shred up used white paper with as little ink as possible (such as large envelopes) or use scraps from a printer.

Collect bundles of paper. Tear into 1-in. squares, place them in a plastic bucket, and cover with water. A full bucket of paper will break down to half a bucket of pulp. Let it soak for at least 24 hours; you can return to the bucket and shred the paper again by hand if you want to break it down more quickly.

You will also need to make a "size" (traditionally gelatin or rosin), which is mixed into the pulp to keep the paper from becoming too porous and making any ink applied to it bleed. Mix two tablespoons of instant starch with two cups of water. Add the starch and water mixture to the bucket containing the mushy paper. You could also mix in two tablespoons of white school glue, which will also act as a size and will help to bond the fibers together.

Next, blend the paper in a food processor, making sure there is enough water to keep the blender from jamming. Run the blender for twenty-second intervals, stopping to rest the motor. The paper is sufficiently pulped when no pieces of paper are visible.

Coloring pulp

To introduce color, add pigment to the pulp in the blender, before the pulp goes into the vat. Or, add color after the paper has been formed on the mesh, by painting or splashing color on.

Colored papers

Dyes already present in colored papers can be used again to color pulp. Fluorescent paper is loaded with dye to give it its intense, vibrant color and the dye will leak out when mixed in the blender with the other pulp. Black paper can be added to the pulp to darken it and paper napkins of solid colors are also useful to color the pulp.

Fabric dyes

Pigments in fabric dyes can be used as colorants. Cold and hot water dyes come with their own fixing agents or mordants that lock in the color. Follow the manufacturer's instructions, apply the dyes to the pulp, and drain the pulp at the end. Metallic fabric paints, hair dyes, shoe dyes, and cosmetic dyes (used in soap making) can be added to tint the pulp. In fact, anything loaded with color will work.

Inks, paints, and food coloring

Inks and paints can be added to the pulp either mixed in evenly with the blender or painted on. While the sheet is wet on a drying board, ink can be blotted, splashed, or sprayed on with a pump action bottle. Ink mixed into the pulp will produce colored paper with a darker colored deckled edge.

Natural dyes

Tea and coffee can be used to make an antique looking paper and is either painted on or mixed into the pulp. Chlorophyll from plants adds a green tinge to the pulp (boiling up spinach or watercress will allow you to extract the green coloring) and herbal teas or boiled petals produces delicate subtle shades.

Kitchen cabinet herbs and spices, such as saffron, turmeric, and paprika, will dye pulp and infuse it with fragrance. Henna can also be used, if soaked in water beforehand.

Bleaching

To extract any color, add a half a cup of household bleach to a bucket half full of pulp and let it stand for four hours, stirring occasionally. Wearing rubber gloves, strain the pulp through a sieve over a bucket and wash the pulp thoroughly with water to clean the bleach out.

Imbedding

Leaves, straws, seaweed, flower petals, and seeds embedded in the paper will not only add flecks of color, but texture too. Silk strands, threads, torn fabric, ripped and shredded papers, sequins, glitters, metallic particles, and crushed mother-of-pearl shells can all be thrown into the pulp in the vat. For a pitted effect sprinkle glitter on the surface of the sheet while it is still on the mold.

Blobs of colored pulp can be embedded into white pulp to create interesting textural effects. You can mix them into the pulp at the blending stage or put blobs directly onto the mold prior to using it in the vat.

Scenting

Adding a drop of essential oil into the pulp will imbue your paper with scent. It is best to scent it after pulping and stir it in well. If you want to scent paper after it has been made, drop some scent on tissues or cotton balls and leave with the paper in a lidded box.

Papermaking

Follow seven simple steps to create your own handmade paper.

❶ Fill the vat two-thirds of the way up with water. Add eight cups of pulp and stir well. The amount of pulp in the water will produce thick or thin papers depending on the quantity of fibers. You will need to add more pulp each time you make a sheet of paper.

❷ Stir the pulp in the vat to make the fibers float. Wet the mold in the vat and then grip the mold and deckle together (with the deckle on the top).

❸ Immerse the mold and deckle vertically, almost to the bottom of the vat, then move them toward you and, still submerged, lift them to a horizontal position. Do this in a curved motion. Slowly raise the frames through the water (picking up the pulp as you lift.) At the top a thin layer of fibers will have formed on the mesh. Rock the frames back and forth and from side to side to even out the settling pulp. This will also help to bond the fibers. Let the water drain from the mold by continuing to hold it over the vat.

4 Tilt the frames to drain out any excess water. Lift the deckle from the mold and move it up and across in a smooth motion to avoid dripping trapped water from the deckle onto the pulp. Drips will create watermarks or patches of thin pulp. If the pulp sticks together or has holes in it, slide it back into the vat, stir it, and start again.

5 Place the mold on a flat surface, with the pulp sheet face up. Press a folded towel onto the pulp and gently blot it. Don't press too hard or wiggle the towel, or you will damage the surface of the sheet. The more water you remove, the stronger the finished sheet will be. You can either leave it to dry on the mold or "couch" it onto another surface.

6 To couch it, spray water from a pump action bottle onto a drying board (use felt instead if you want a textured surface). The board or felt needs to be wet so that the sheet will stick to it. Turn the mold over onto your wet board and press on the back of the mesh with a dry sponge. Keep pressing, squeezing out your sponge, until you have removed all the excess water you can. Lift the mold from the board, leaving the sheet behind.

7 It is best to dry the sheet indoors as sun or heat can shrink the paper. The amount of time it takes to dry will depend on the fibers, thickness, and temperature of the room. It can take twelve hours or up to two days. When the paper has dried it begins to rise slightly at the edges. Use a flat blade to gently pry it off the board. If it is still wet on the underside, sandwich it between dry felt or dish towels and place hardback books on top as a weight to stop it from curling up. When you have six or more dry sheets of paper, put them between hardback books to keep them flat until you want to use them.

Texturing, Casting, Molding, and Waterproofing

Texturing

The surface of wet paper can be textured with items such as tops of pens and plastic combs. Any rounded (not sharp) object can be used to change the surface. Alternatively, make a rough pulp (by leaving pieces of paper in it) to create a textured surface.

To texture with a comb

Make a sheet of paper from a thick pulp and couch it onto a drying board. Wet a plastic wide-toothed comb and use it to ruffle the surface without breaking it. Sweep it one way only and leave to dry.

Casting

Thick pulp can be poured or squashed over items such as foam shapes, shells, and pebbles.

To make a cast:

❶ Start by soaking pulp in water with white school glue. It is best to leave it for several hours.

❷ Position the item you want to cast (here a piece of foam is used) on the drying board and cover it with pieces of pulp until it isn't visible anymore. If there are any weak areas, cover them with more pulp.

❸ Press the pulp with a mesh or piece of silk-screen cloth. Blot the excess water from the mesh with a sponge.

❹ Allow to dry on the board for 24 hours. Peel the paper upward, removing the foam.

 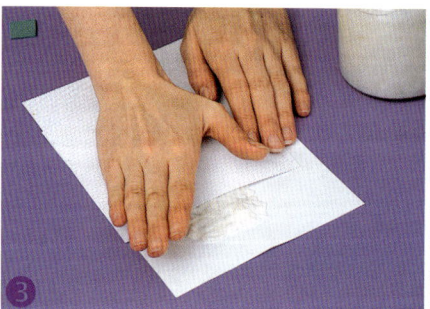 

Molding

Leftover wet pulp (mixed with plenty of white school glue) acts as papier-mâché that can be molded into any shape. When dry it is very light and can be painted with acrylic or poster paint. For the "Grandparents" project (page 58), simple balls were used to finish the handle of the plant holder. To make them, follow these two easy steps:

❶ Take a handful of pulp and squeeze out as much water as possible (to aid drying) and then roll it into balls in the palms of your hands.

❷ Pierce all the way through the ball to make chunky beads that can be painted and threaded when dry.

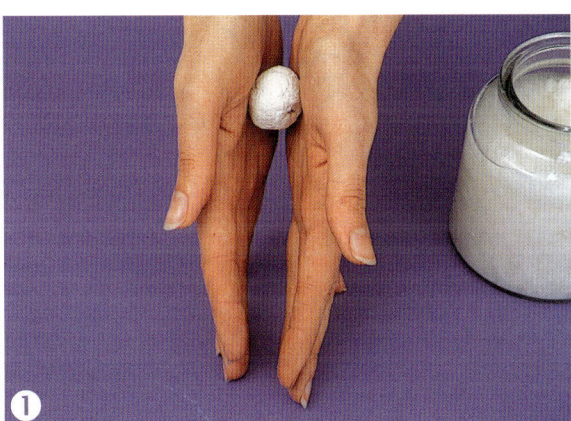
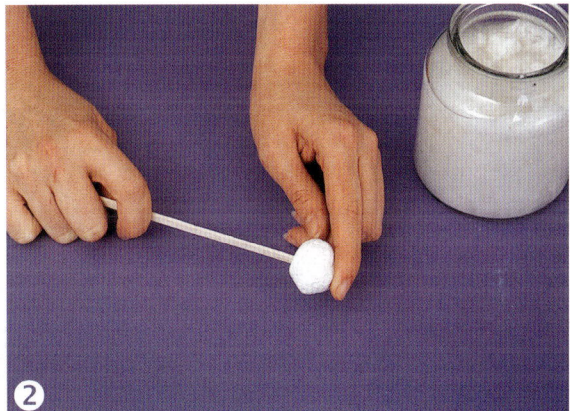

Waterproofing

To make tissue paper waterproof, you can use wax. Melt a beeswax candle in a heatproof dish in the microwave. To keep the wax from getting too hot and bubbling up, melt it at ten-second intervals. With an oven mitt, move the dish with the melted wax to a metal sink with ¾ in. of cold water in the bottom of it. Dip tissue paper into the wax repeatedly until all the paper is covered. Then, dip the waxed paper into the cold water to harden. Once the wax has hardened, any water will run off it and the paper is effectively waterproof.

Choosing Paper and Card

There are quite simply thousands of varieties of paper available from all over the world. Listed here are some of the ones you are more likely to encounter in specialized paper shops, stationers, and craft stores. Papers can be inspiring in themselves; collect them and keep them flat between two sheets of mounting board until you decide what you want to use them for.

Handmade and natural papers

There are a wide variety of handmade papers available—most are from North India and Thailand. Some have beautiful textures, opulent colors, or exotic leaves, petals, and seeds embedded in them. They can be heavy in weight or very light and fine and are generally about the same size as a sheet of wrapping paper. There are four types of commercially available handmade paper used in this book:

Khadi or cotton rag paper, from India, is often made from waste such as scraps of cotton t-shirts left over from the fashion industry. It is a dense paper that is great for folding and scoring.

Lokta is paper of a medium weight that has lots of long fibers in its structure. It is smooth with a slightly shiny surface making it suitable for rubber-stamping. It is made in the Himalayas from the bark of the lokta tree.

Mulberry is used to make a variety of papers of different densities. The lighter papers are opaque when held up to the light, and the fibers and strawlike fronds from mulberry trees are clearly visible. Most mulberry papers come from Thailand or Japan.

Lace papers are very light, flimsy papers also made from mulberry. They have gaps in between the fibers to create the look of lace. Forcing water through a patterned screen onto newly formed sheets creates the gaps. They are made in Japan and may be referred to as washi—"wa" means "Japanese" and "shi" means "paper."

Tissue, crepe, and honeycomb

Tissue is a very light paper often used for wrapping gifts. One sheet may be transparent, so to make it less see-through use several sheets.

Crepe paper is great for wrapping things, as its wrinkled surface has an elastic quality and will mold itself around objects. It can be a single color, two-toned, or metallic.

Honeycomb paper is made from tissue papers that have been fused together. If you

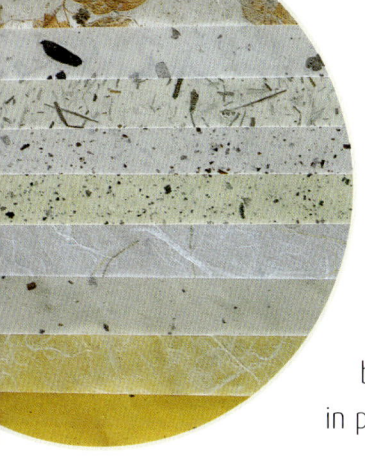

pull the outer layers of tissue apart they will open up to reveal a honeycomb-like network.

Translucent papers are like tracing papers in opacity and weight, but can be brightly colored and still retain their see-through quality. They are also available in pastel hues and can have pearly or metallic finishes.

Plain paper and **card** are made from wood pulp and reclaimed wood pulp. They are available in different weights and sizes and a kaleidoscope of colors. They are a great staple paper to make into cards or to use for decoration, and can be smooth or textured.

Gloss, **metallic**, **pearlescent**, and **holographic card** are made from plain card that has been coated with varnish to give a glossy or metallic appearance. Some white gloss boards can be used for rubber-stamping and embossing to great effect. The best card to use for this is Astrolux or Chromolux.

Mounting board is a bonded sheet of bleached wood pulp, sandwiched between two sheets of colored paper. It is a stiff board, which can be cut with a knife and used for picture framing.

Watercolor paper is heavy, textured paper, usually white or off-white, that is specially made to use with watercolor paints. The weight and texture mean it won't buckle and wrinkle when wet. The more expensive varieties are made from cotton pulp and are watermarked or embossed with the maker's name.

Wallpaper works well as a craft material, as it is strong and durable and is easy to cut and fold. Wallpapers can be printed, plain, or embossed and can look really effective.

Envelopes

When making cards, it is a good idea to have an envelope size in mind. You will want the envelope to be about ¼ in. bigger than the card so it will fit well.

Equipment Needed

Cutting equipment

Scissors
Razor knife
Flexible steel ruler
Cutting mat (to protect surfaces)

Cutting equipment, such as scissors and a razor knife, are a must for crafting paper. If you are making a blank card, mark the center of the card and score down it with a metal ruler and your thumb nail (this will make folding it easier). A flexible ruler will accommodate handmade paper and bumpy surfaces. A cutting mat allows you to use a knife without cutting through to the table underneath. Cutting windows with a knife requires a little practice. Start with the points of the window so you don't overcut.

Making holes

Hole punch (single)
Hole punch (double)
Rivet tool (enclosed in packet of rivets) and hammer
Craft punches of mixed designs
Bookbinding pricker

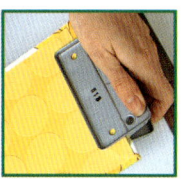

Hole punches are really useful tools to collect. They make perfect holes, unlike trying to make holes with scissor blades. Craft punches are quick to use and can be bought in hundreds of different shapes. A bookbinding pricker is great for making small holes in layers of paper or thick card.

Adhesives

White school glue
Glue stick
Strong glue
Sticky foam pads
Double-sided adhesive tape

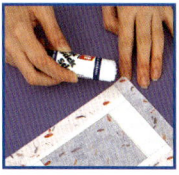

There are five types of adhesive that should meet all your needs. White school glue is slow-drying glue, which goes on white and dries clear. It can be used as a size in papermaking (making paper impervious to ink) and can be painted on paper to give a varnished look. Glue sticks, foam pads, and double-sided adhesive tape will join lighter papers and card together. Stronger glue is needed to join other materials, such as metal, to paper.

Drawing and coloring materials

Pencil
Colored pencils
Fine line pen
Felt-tip pens
Marker pen
Dip pen
Paint brushes: stenciling brush, fine brushes

A basic selection of pens, pencils, and paints are used throughout the book. A stenciling brush is useful and is cheap to buy. It can be used for lots of different applications where you require a big brush.

Reproducing images

Tracing paper
Rubber stamps and stamp pads
Foam (for making own stamps)
Plastic (for stencil)
Photocopier, PC, and printer
Letter transfers

Tracing paper can be used to transfer images. Lay it on top of an image, copy the edge with a pencil, flip the tracing paper over, and scribble on the back. Turn the tracing over again and lay on card, retrace around the original pencil line, and the image will transfer.

Foam is a useful material, as it is water resistant and can be used to make your own basic stamps (an updated version of the potato print). A sheet of thin transparent plastic (or polypropylene) can be used to make stencils. Scraps can be used as paint palettes or glue spreaders.

Enlarging and reducing images is tricky without the aid of a photocopier and you will need to use one for enlarging the templates at the back of the book.

Embellishments

Finding embellishments to use with paper is a fun hobby in itself. Collect materials that inspire you. Look in craft shops, clothing stores, junk shops, markets, or even in the park.

Coloring

Acrylic pots

Watercolor

Inks and pipette bottle

Tea and coffee

Material paint in gold

Fabric glitter paint in tube

Dye for coloring paper

Craft sticks

Stamping and stenciling

Ink pads in gold, lilac, red

Gold acrylic

Embossing stamp and powder

Scraps of foam and plastic to make stamps and stencils

Sewing and threading materials

Threads

Needles

Pearl-headed pins

Crochet thread

Ribbons

Black cord elastic

Silk strands

Squares of net and fabrics

Thread

Needles

Crochet thread

Ribbons

Black cord elastic

Silk strands

Embellishments

Confetti shapes

Sequins with holes (to allow them to be stitched)

Glitter and sequin shakers

Pressed flowers and leaves

Sparkle stones

Dot stickers

Shape stickers

Wiggly eyes

Fabric flowers

Paper shapes cut from craft punches

Seed beads

Bookbinders and eyelets

¼ in. brass screw binders

½ in. brass screw binders

Brass eyelets

White metal and colored eyelets (and tool)

Wax and matches

Wax candle (for waterproofing tissue paper)

Sealing wax in gold and bronze

Initial seals

Lettering

Torn letters from magazines

Pen nibs

Jewelry accessories

Bobby pins

Pin backs

Part Two: Crafting

Personal Events

Add a personal touch by creating something unique for events such as weddings, anniversaries, and the birth of new babies. This section contains special cards and gifts for all these occasions.

A New Home

Stained-glass window and card by Ella Cheqwyn. Lamp shade by Emma Angel.

This card or lamp shade project will enable you to make the perfect gift to celebrate moving into a new home. It will appeal to everyone from homeowners to apartment dwellers.

The window is made from layers of paper and could be altered to match specific color schemes. It works superbly due to the opaque nature of some papers. When light streams through it, you can see the structure of the paper, petals, strands, and fronds. The holes made by stitching are also illuminated and the colors glow and cast mellow tones onto surrounding walls.

To make the lamp shade you will need a frame to wrap the paper around. You could either salvage one from a flea market, by tearing it out of an existing lamp shade, or purchase one from a specialized craft shop. Here a square frame is used to maintain the architectural theme. If you wanted to eliminate stitching the panels together, you could use a round frame.

You will need:

    White card x 2 (for the template and front panel)
    Knife and cutting mat
    Ruler
    Pieces of mixed papers and scraps of fabrics such as net
      or lace, scraps of foils, and candy wrappers
    Glue stick
    Sewing machine and thread
    Measuring tape
    Metal lamp shade frame
    Scissors
    White handmade paper
    Strong glue
    Craft sticks

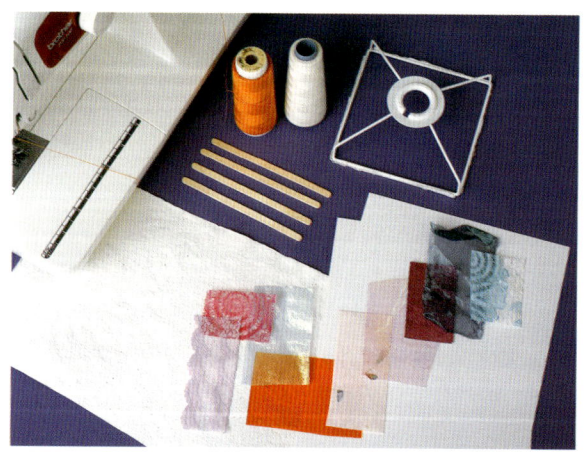

To make the lamp shade:

First you will need to make a church window by making a template.

1 Draw a template of church windows onto a sheet of white card.

2 Cut out the windows. A ruler can be used for the straight edges.

3 Layer mixed pieces of paper over the windows. Secure them to the white card with a glue stick.

4 Turn the paper over and stitch around the windows using a sewing machine with colored thread.

5 Stitch all the way around, not forgetting the middle sections.

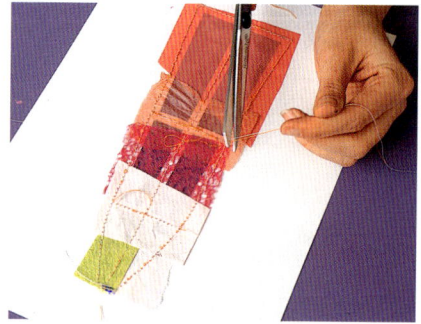

6 Pull threads through to the back when finished. Cut off any surplus papers or threads.

Measure your frame. The one used here is 5½ in. square. If your frame is larger, adjust the measurements to fit, not forgetting to add a ¼ in. seam allowance on either side.

To make a card:

The same stained-glass window can be used to make a tall, skinny greeting card. Cut white card to 9½ by 12 in., score, and fold it in half to make a blank card. Follow steps 1 to 6 on the inside of the card.

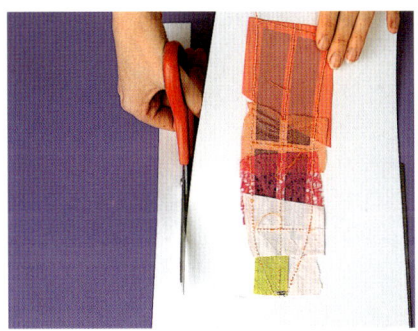

7 Cut the sheet 6¼ in. across and 11 in. long, making sure the window is central.

8 To make the other panels, cut three sheets of handmade white paper 6¼ by 11 in.

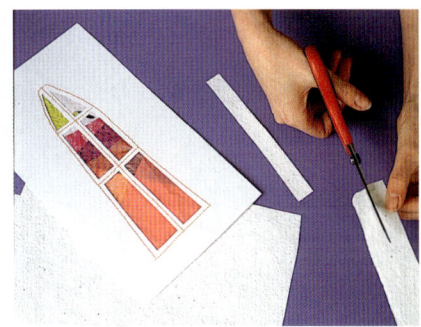

9 From the same paper, cut two thin strips ¾ by 6¼ in.

10 Stitch the two strips to the top and bottom of the front panel to strengthen it.

11 Stitch all the oblong panels together by overlapping the allowances. Sew all four panels together to form a strip with the window sheet second from the left. Fold along the stitching to form a box shape.

12 Flatten the paper and glue craft sticks along the bottom edge to reinforce it. Cut the sticks down to size if they are too long.

13 (Left) Apply strong glue to the metal frame and wrap the paper around it. Make sure the corners meet.

14 (Right) Fold the final allowance over and glue it to complete your shade.

Baby

Bouncing baby card and mobile.

What better way of celebrating the birth of a new baby than by making a card and mobile to hang above the crib. Baby cards don't have to be all pastels and storks. Make a boldly colored card for the arrival of a new baby and it will stand out from the others. Use non-gender-specific colors such as green, purple, red, and orange.

Here paw prints and dogs were used to decorate the card and mobile, but you don't have to use this design. You could make a foam stamp of a fish or rabbit or make caricatures of other family pets. A colorful mobile hanging over the baby's crib will give him or her happy dreams of furry friends.

You will need:
Green card
Knife and cutting mat
Pencil
Ruler
For the paw print stamp:
  Foam rubber
  Glue
  Block of wood or plastic
    box top
  Black acrylic paint
Purple card
Glue stick
Black fiber-tip pen
Thin white card
Colored felt-tip pens: pink,
  red, orange
Scissors
Needle and thread

1 Score and fold a sheet of green card in half to form a blank card. Inside the card, mark out a window using a pencil and ruler. Draw a horizontal line 1¼ in. from the top and a line 1¼ in. from the bottom. Draw two vertical lines 1 in. in from the edges. Cut diagonally from the corners of the window with a knife. Cut the remaining card out of the frame. Keep the triangles to use later for the mobile.

2 Make a paw-shaped stamp by cutting three small circles and one larger one from foam. Glue the paws onto a plastic box top or block of wood. Paint over the stamp with black acrylic. Stamp onto a piece of purple paper to test. Keep this for later use in the mobile.

3 With the card frame opened out flat, cover the left side of the card with a spare sheet of paper to protect the back from splashes of paint. Stamp the paw print onto the card frame randomly, repainting it with acrylic when necessary. Leave to dry.

7 Cut the baby out. Thread a needle and knot the end of the thread. Stitch through the baby's head.

8 Stitch through the center of the frame. Pull the threads to the desired length and knot in a loop.

4 Cut a sheet of purple card into a 5 by 7-in. piece to line the inside of the card. Stick it to the inside with a glue stick.

5 Draw a cute baby wearing a t-shirt onto a scrap of white paper. Trace the baby onto thin, white card. Using a thick marker pen draw over the pencil lines. The ink will show through the thin card, allowing you to mark the outlines on the reverse.

6 Color the baby in with felt-tip pens. Here they were colored roughly with scribbling motions. Color the two sides differently. Here one side was colored red and one side orange, with a paw print on one side and a dog on the other.

To make the mini mobile:

9 Cut out two circles with paw prints in the center on purple card and two circles with dogs on red card. Glue them together.

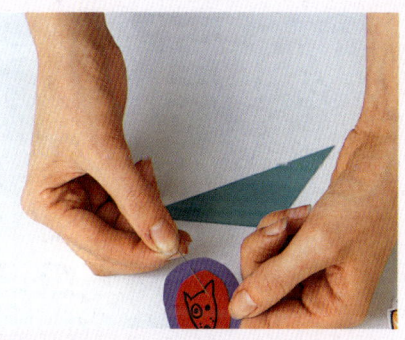

10 Make the baby as before. Using needle and thread you can sew the paw prints and baby to a leftover triangle (from making the window). Stitch the baby to the center point of the triangle with the paws on either side. Stitch a loop for hanging. Make sure the mobile hangs level before you knot the ends.

Wedding

Bridal "bodice" keepsake box, card, and confetti.

This wedding project has a romantic, fairy-tale look created from card, ribbon, a bodice stamp, and a Jordan almond color scheme of lilac, white, and pink.

    The keepsake box can be used to store wedding cards after the big day. It is laced with lashings of white ribbon to continue the theme of the rubber stamp, and the matching card is also threaded with ribbon, so that the bride has to untie it to open it.

    To give the bodice the effect of raised embroidery, embossing powders were used. You can mix them together to match the bride's color scheme.

    Confetti made from translucent papers and craft punches decorate the front of the box and the card. The shapes are glued on randomly to create the look of a fluttering shower of confetti and sparkle stones add a glint of diamond to the decorations. Don't forget to make some extra confetti to throw at the wedding.

You will need:

- Craft punches: dove, cherub, hearts, and flowers
- Mixed translucent papers
- Bodice rubber stamp
- Embossing stamp pad
- Embossing powder
- White glossy card
- Toaster
- Glue stick or strong glue
- Sparkle stones
- Pale pink card
- White card
- Pencil and ruler
- Single hole punch
- Eyelets
- White ribbon

To make confetti:

1 Cut confetti by punching out lots of shapes from a mixture of translucent papers. Put several sheets together to make the process quicker. Keep punching until you have a handful.

To stamp the bodice:

2 Cover the rubber stamp with embossing ink, making sure it is completely covered.

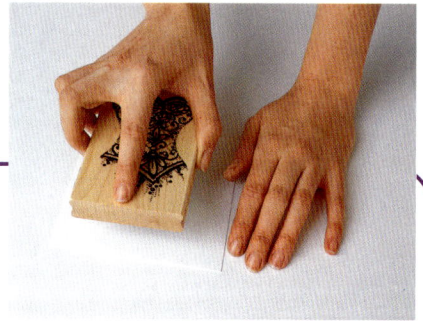

3 Stamp it down on a square of gloss card. Lift off smoothly without wiggling it and spoiling the design.

4 Sprinkle with embossing powder. To make it easy to put surplus back in the bottle, sprinkle it inside a folded piece of paper. This way you can shake the powder into the crease and pour it back in the bottle.

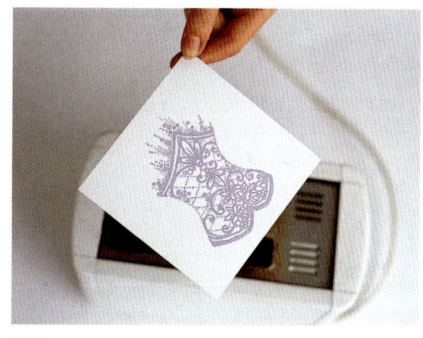

5 Using an old toaster, heat the underside of the card. Move the card around and watch for the powder to melt and become raised.

6 Glue randomly scattered confetti shapes to the card. Glue on sparkle stones too.

To make the box:

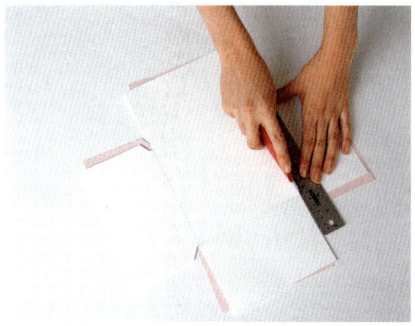

7 Copy the template of the box from the back of the book onto white and pink card. Make the top pink and the bottom white. Cut out, score, and fold along the lines.

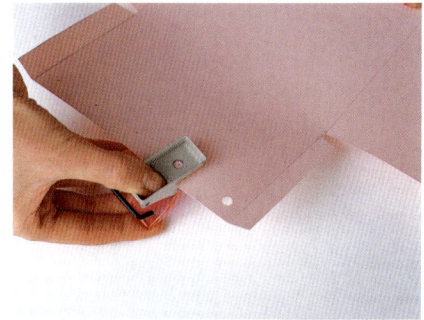

8 Leave the pink box top flat so you can mark holes for the eyelets. Mark four evenly spaced dots along two of the edges. Using the hole punch turned upside down, punch out holes where the dots are.

9 Slot in the eyelets and hammer them down, using the tool provided in the packet.

10 Assemble the box by folding along the lines and gluing along the tabs using a glue stick or stronger glue.

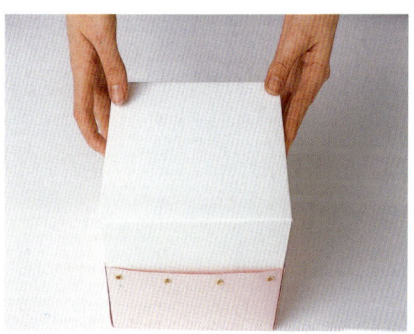

11 Slide the top of the box over the bottom.

12 Thread white ribbon through the eyelets, criss-crossing it over the top of the box. Place the square previously decorated with the bodice stamp and confetti on top of the box under the ribbons.

To make a matching greeting card:

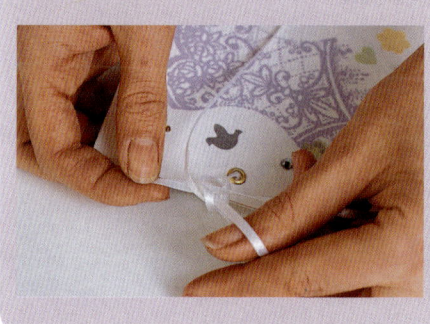

13 Cut an oblong of glossy card 9¾ by 5 in. and fold in half to form a blank card. Follow steps 1 to 6 to decorate the front. Make eyelets at the front and back of the card. Thread with ribbon and tie in a bow.

Bon Voyage Book

Exotic journal.

This exotic journal is made from stitching attractive papers together. It isn't necessary to spend years learning bookbinding skills to create something beautiful. Simple stitching is effective enough for this project.

The book can be given to a friend who is embarking on far-flung travels or used as a scrapbook for previous holidays. For the leaves of the book, make your own papers embedded with treasures you have brought back from holidays. Fragments of packaging, petals, spices, threads, or even plane tickets can be thrown into the pulp. The finished papers will act as reminders of places you have visited. Team them with opulent marbled papers or papers you may have collected. Seek inspiration from journeys to the exotic East, for example, and create a book that will be a feast for the senses with varied textures, scented pages, and vivid colors. Try to stick to a loose color scheme so that your book looks eclectic rather than a mess. Here purples, pinks, and golds are used. Gold ink and a rubber stamp of baggage labels have been used to decorate the cover and some of the pages.

You will need:

- Rubber stamp of luggage labels
- Gold ink pad
- Lokta paper in purple
- White card for the cover 12¼ by 9 in.
- Glue stick
- Sheet of paper to cover the inside
- For the leaves: a collection of papers of various sizes
- Pencil and ruler
- Bookbinding pricker
- Darning needle
- Gold crochet thread

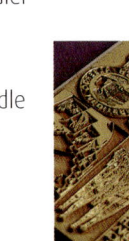

To make the cover and the leaves:

1 Use the stamp to make a gold pattern on the shiny side of a sheet of purple lokta paper. Turn it in various directions to give the pattern a random look. Allow the ink to dry.

2 To make the cover, rub a glue stick on the white card and lay it on the reverse side of the stamped paper. Rub the surface to iron out any wrinkles. Cut the stamped paper to 11 by 14 in. to cover the card. Fold the paper and card in half to make a crease and open it out.

3 Fold in the corners of the covering paper inward and glue them down.

7 Open the leaves out and lay them inside the cover. You will need to make five marks along the fold for the holes. Measure ⅞ in. from the top of the pages and make a pencil mark. Mark 1 in. up from the bottom. Mark 1½ in. in from both the marks you have already made. Make a final mark in the middle.

8 Use the pricker to make holes through the pages and through the cover. Push right through all of the marks.

9 With a needle and crochet thread, stitch through the holes, starting from the middle of the cover, leaving a long thread behind. Come up through the pages and stitch to the next hole. You need to make a figure eight with the thread, starting and finishing in the middle.

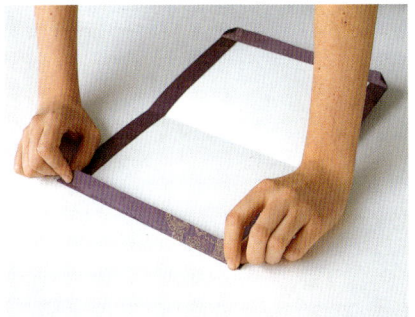

4 Rub glue along all the edges and fold inward onto the back of the cover.

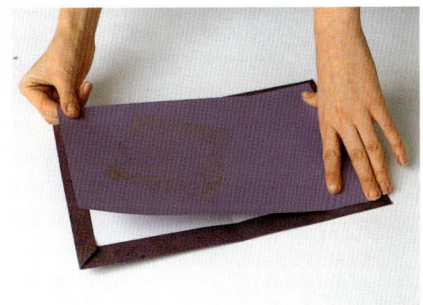

5 Now that the card is covered, glue a sheet of lining paper inside it. This could be stamped or plain.

6 Fold sheets together to form the leaves of the book. For an unusual variation, fold some square sheets diagonally.

10 Repeat this until all the holes are stitched and you are back to the middle again. Stitch back through the middle hole so your thread is on the outside.

11 Tie the threads together. You can leave the end long to wrap around the book to close it or tie a bow and cut them short.

Notebooks

You could make some smaller stitched books that could be used as notebooks. Pierce the covers with the pricking tool and put the stitching outside of the book rather than through the spine. Cardboard folded to create a ridge is used to make hardback books. Experiment with making hardback and paperback books of varying sizes, colors, and textures. They will make unusual gifts, although you may not want to give them away.

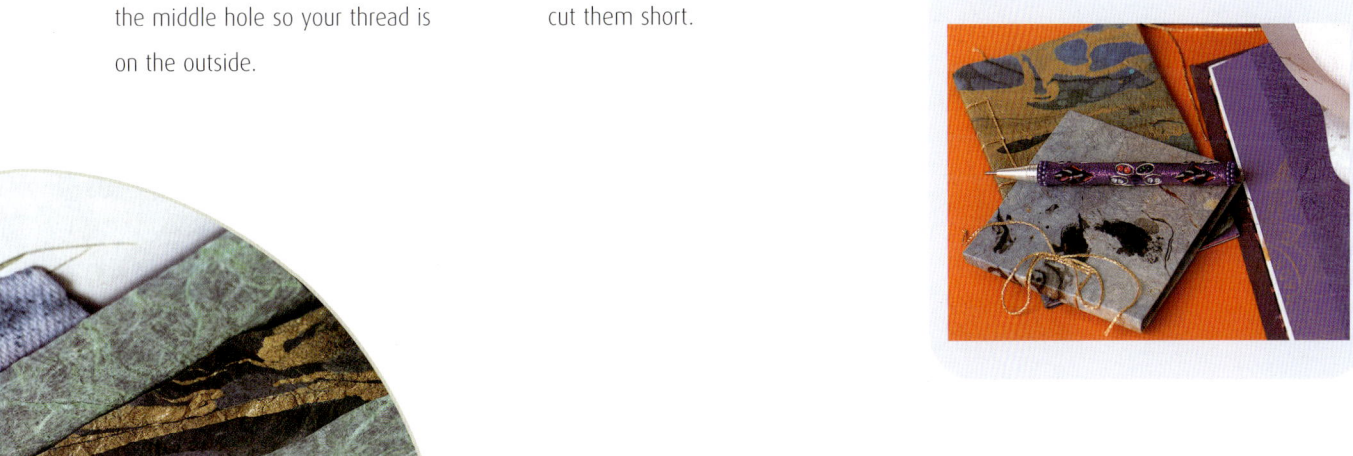

Anniversary

Antiqued anniversary card by Emma Angel and Louise McSweeney.

This glamorous card would be great to send to an older female relative or as an anniversary card. We've used a nostalgic image from a 1930s magazine, but you could use an old wedding photo or a collage made from decoupage scraps.

The card is three sided and is "aged" using tea and coffee, which is a simple but very effective technique. The finished card incorporates crackle-glazed hearts, gold peel-off stickers, and a handwritten message using an old-fashioned dip pen and sepia ink. As an extra-special touch you could close the envelope with a blob of fragrant sealing wax, imprinting it with an initial seal.

It is an old European tradition (dating back to medieval Germany) to send certain gifts for each anniversary, for example, paper for the first anniversary and cotton for the second. You could match your card's theme to match the gift it is traditional to send. Here gold trimmings are used, but you could use bronze, ruby, or silver or add hearts cut from materials such as cotton, lace, linen, leather, or wood to stay in keeping with the anniversary. A pressed flower, small pottery ornament, pearl, or crystal beads could also be added to the card to adapt it.

You will need:
- Textured cream card (to make the blank card)
- Scissors
- Pencil and ruler
- Tea bag
- Instant coffee granules
- Knife and cutting mat
- Gold peel-off stickers
- Gold card
- Crackle glaze
- White acrylic paint
- Glue stick
- An image from a vintage magazine, old photo, or decoupage scraps

To decorate (optional):
- Dip pen and sepia ink
- Gold sealing wax and seal

To make the blank card:

1 To make the three-sided blank card, cut an oblong of card 12¼ by 6 in. Score and fold it 4⅛ in. in from the edge and again at 8⅛ in. To age the card, dip a tea bag in a cup of just boiled water. Using a thick brush, paint tea onto the card.

2 Drop instant coffee granules onto the card while still wet. These will dissolve, leaving a speckled effect. Allow to dry overnight.

3 Cut out templates of hearts: one big, 2¼ in. from tip to bow, and one smaller heart, 2 in. from tip to bow. Position the big heart on the front fold with the bow 1¼ in. from the top of the card. Position the smaller heart 1½ in. from the top of the back fold. Measure them to make sure the centers of the hearts are level so that the windows will be centered. Draw around the hearts. Leave the middle of the card empty.

To crackle glaze the hearts:

6 Cut two or more hearts from the gold card.

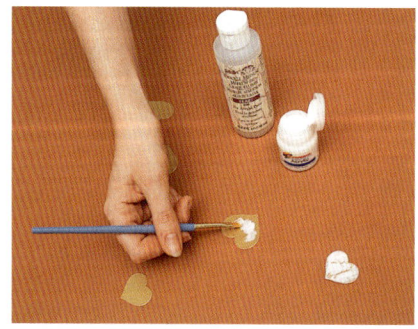

7 Age them by painting on crackle glaze. Leave the glaze to dry. Paint over the top with white acrylic. Cracks will begin to appear as the two mediums react.

8 To decorate the card you could also write "Happy Anniversary" on a scrap of cream card using an old-fashioned dip pen and sepia ink.

4 Cut out the heart on a cutting mat with the knife starting with the points. Push out.

5 Decorate the card with peel-off stickers along the border and fold it inward.

9 On the back wall of the card, glue an image, photo, or decoupage scraps.

10 Collage together the card, hearts, and wording. Glue together.

You could seal the envelope with melted gold sealing wax. Melt wax directly onto the flap and press down with the initial seal.

Get Well Soon

Get-well pinwheels.

Bright, colorful pinwheels will make great "get well soon" presents or could be given as "cheer up" gifts. Super stripes and dotty spots are reminiscent of the deck chairs and windbreakers of beach vacations. You will need to paint them onto paper rather than card to allow the windmill to be light enough to spin around. Stripes can be a mixture of wide and narrow widths. Here a green pencil has been used to add some thin stripes too. The dots can be little dabs or large sunny circles.

The pinwheels are surprisingly easy to make; you could make huge ones and tiny ones by enlarging or reducing the template at the back of the book.

You will need:
> Scissors
> Red paper
> Pale green paper
> Paintbrush
> Acrylic paint in red and
>   orange
> Green colored pencil
> Pencil and ruler
> Card
> Hole punch (single)
> ½ in. brass screw binders
> Craft sticks or the like
> Strong glue

**For the mini pinwheel
you will also need:**
> Pale green curling ribbon
> Pearl-headed pin

get well soon

get well soon

To make the pinwheel:

❶ Cut two squares of paper 5¾ by 5¾ in. Cut one red and one pale green square. Paint stripes on the pale green paper and use the green pencil to draw finer lines. Dab orange dots on the red paper. Leave to dry.

❷ Trace the template at the back of the book onto card. Punch out holes and cut around. Mark an "F" for the front, flip it over and mark a "B" for the back.

❸ Trace template "F" onto the back of the red square.

❼ Twist the top sheet around so that the red sheet fits into the gaps. Slot the corner holes over the screw binder working your way around.

❽ Screw the top of the brass binder down when complete.

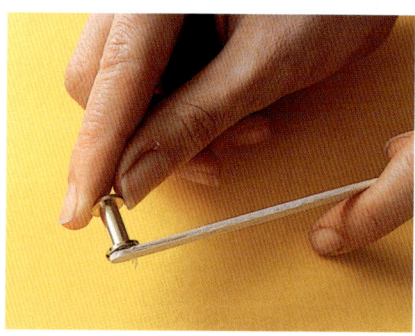

❾ Glue another brass binder onto a craft stick with strong glue.

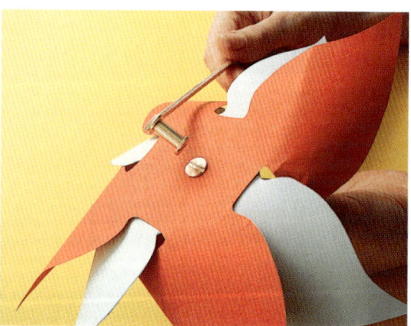

❿ Glue on the back to form a spoke to enable the pinwheel to rotate.

4 Trace template "B" onto the back of the green paper.

5 Punch out holes and cut around both of the pieces.

6 Lay the two pieces together with the stripes on the top and the dots on the bottom. Make a hole in the center (either by using an eyelet device or by pushing a scissor blade through). Then push a screw binder through the center.

Mini pinwheel

1 Instead of giving someone a "get well" card, you could make a mini pinwheel and a striped box to stand it in. You can paint "get well" on some green curling ribbon with acrylic paint and thread it onto the back of the pinwheel. Here a pearl-headed pin is pushed through the paper, stick, and ribbon to join them together.

2 You will need to bend the pin over, on the back, to secure everything.

BIRTHDAYS

Have you ever noticed whatever time of the year it is, it always seems to be somebody's birthday? The next section has card and gift-wrapping ideas to suit friends and family. Different ages, from young boys and girls to grandparents, are creatively catered to in this section. All you need now are the gifts.

Birthday Boy

Creepy, crawly caterpillar.

These fun, silly cards made from honeycomb paper will appeal to young boys. They will approve of the funny-faced caterpillar, munching his way out of the apple, even if they don't like eating fruit themselves.

Boys love slugs, snails, and creepy crawlies, and they also love candy. In this project the two are combined in the form of a creepy, crawly, candy caterpillar.

Purple, red, yellow, and green are combined for a simple, bold look, but the red "honeycomb" apple could be changed to a green or yellow pear, an orange, or even a pineapple.

You will need:
    Purple card
    White card
    Pencil
    Red honeycomb paper
    Scissors
    Red card
    Glue stick
    2 packages of dot stickers:
      1 large and 1 small
      (available from office
      supply stores)
    Wiggly eyes
    Black pen
    Green paper

To make the card:

❶ Fold a small piece of purple card in half.

❷ Draw half an apple shape onto the card to make a template.

❸ Draw half an apple onto honeycomb paper across the grain of the paper.

❼ Glue one side of the apple to the purple card 1 in. down. Stretch the apple across and glue the other side to the card.

❽ Stick on yellow and green dots to make the caterpillar. Overlap them to form sections of his body.

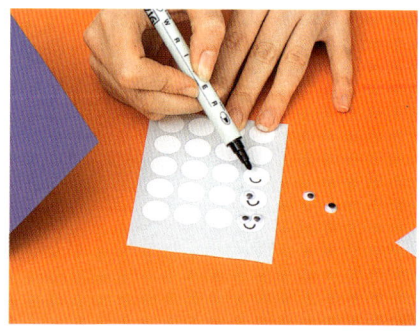

❾ Make a face using a white dot sticker, wiggly eyes, and black pen.

To make the caterpillar:

You will need:

Yellow crepe paper
6 round candies or gumballs
Yellow pipe cleaners
Scissors
Green tissue
Scraps of white and black paper
Glue stick
Dot stickers
Wiggly eyes
Black pen

The caterpillar is made from crepe and tissue papers and large round candy. You could always wrap up bouncy balls or marbles if you prefer.

Lay an oblong piece of crepe paper down on a flat surface. Evenly space the items about 1 in. from the edge and roll the edge inward and over the

4 Cut the apple from the red honey-comb paper.

5 Cut two apple halves from red card.

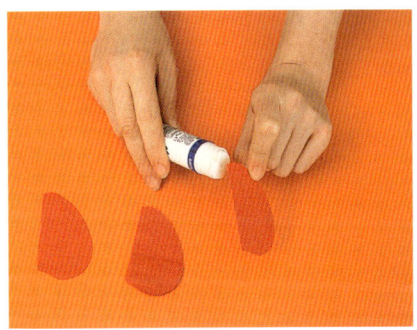

6 Glue them to the honeycomb apple using a glue stick.

10 Stick the face onto the caterpillar's body.

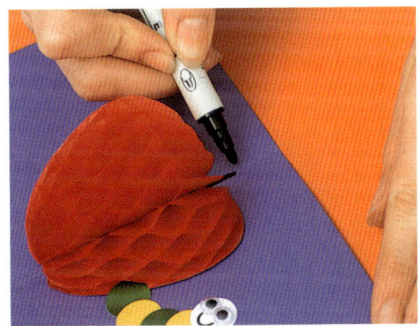

11 Draw a black stalk above the apple along the fold of the card.

12 Stick on two smaller yellow dots above the caterpillar's face for anten-nae. Join the head and antennae together with the black pen.

balls. Keep rolling carefully until all the paper has been used. Wiggle the balls around if they have moved out of place. Secure one end by tightly wrap-ping a pipe cleaner around it. Cut the pipe cleaner down to create little legs. Cut a strip of green tissue paper and wrap that around the second section

and tie with a pipe cleaner on either side. Do the same all the way along until you reach the end.
Flatten out the end of the paper and glue a disk of white paper to the end to make a friendly face. Make antennae by sticking dots to strips of black paper. Glue on wiggly eyes and draw a smile.

13 Cut out a double leaf shape from a folded piece of green paper and glue it onto the card, just above the apple.

Birthday Girl

Glitter girl.

Candy-colored cards will appeal to a young girl's sensibility. You can glam up the pink card with iridescent glitter to create scrumptious, shimmering cards. Decorate bobby pins with white fabric flowers and sparkle stones to incorporate into the card. Little princesses will love these fashionable cards and can wear the bobby pins too.

You will need to make color photocopies of the face from the picture shown below. Make it 2¼ in. long (from chin to forehead). Alternatively, you can draw your own fashionable girl or make a caricature of the recipient.

You could also make a cool badge using the same technique as for the card. Or make a card and thread a bracelet behind a color-copied girl to make her look as if she is wearing a long necklace.

You will need:
- White school glue
- Iridescent glitter
- Pink card
- Stenciling paintbrush
- Sheet of plastic
- Pencil
- Scissors
- Sheet of color-copied faces
- Fuchsia pink foam
- Glue stick
- Fabric daisy trim
- Bobby pins
- Sparkle stones
- Peel-off plastic
- Pin back

To make the card:

1 Mix white school glue and glitter together.

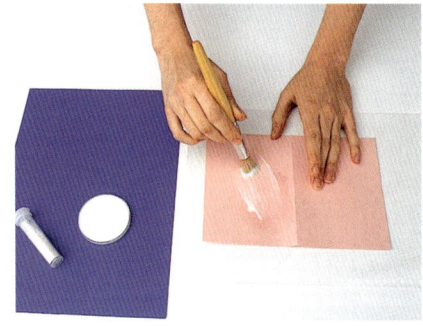

2 Lay a pink card on a piece of plastic and paint the glitter and glue mixture on the front and back. Leave to dry on the plastic overnight.

3 Make a hair template on a scrap of card and cut around it.

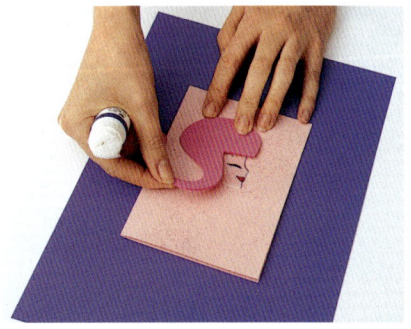

7 Glue the cut-out hair on top of the face, making sure the face is still visible.

8 Cut fabric daisies from a piece of trim. Glue them onto two plain bobby pins.

9 Add a sparkle stone to the center of the flower with a dab of glue.

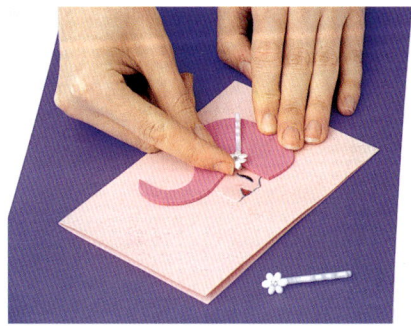

10 Push one of the bobby pins diagonally onto the foam hair. Push it along until the flower is in the corner. Slide the other pin alongside it.

④ Copy the template onto fuchsia pink foam using a pencil.

⑤ Cut along the line smoothly without making too many little snips. This will keep the edge smooth.

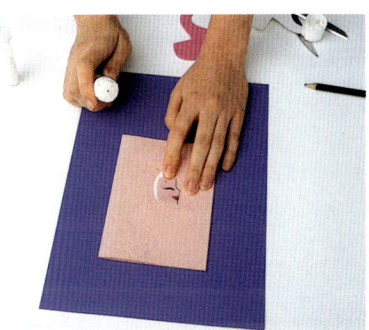

⑥ Cut around a color-copied face. Position it slightly off center to allow for the hair. Glue it to the sparkly card using a glue stick.

To make a badge:

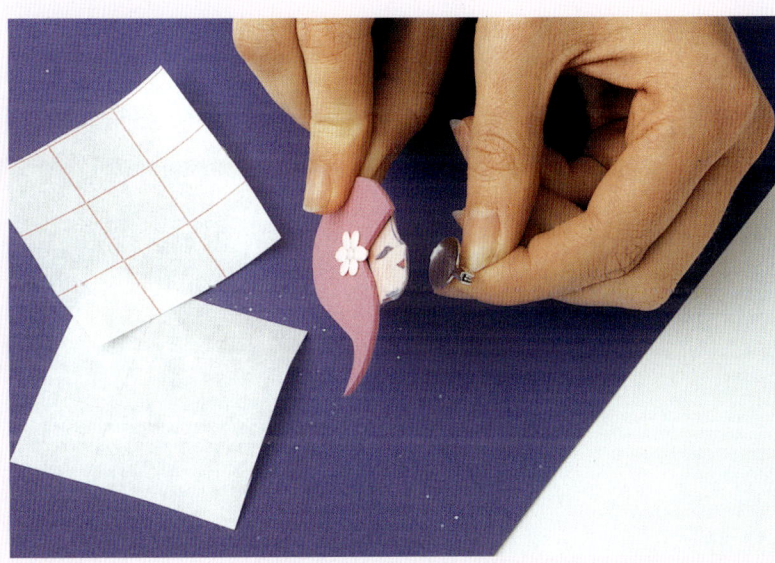

Wrapping paper idea!

You could paint some pink tissue paper with white school glue and glitter to create matching sparkly wrapping paper.

Make a color photocopy of the girl (with body). Cut around her face. Cut a hair shape from foam that is larger than the face. Laminate the back and front of the face with peel-off plastic to make it waterproof so that it can be worn. Glue the face onto the foam hair and glue on one of the flowers and sparkle stone. Glue on the pin back with some strong glue. Once the glue has dried the badge can be worn to glamorous effect.

Teens

Pop Star card and CD holder by Debbie Webb.

For this project you can make a card and a CD holder. Teens and preteens will love them. Shiny, metallic, and glossy white cards are combined with acetate for a slick, space-age look. Silver star sequins are trapped in between the layers and when the card is shaken, the stars will move for a dazzling, disco effect.

You can alter the Pop Star slogan to fit the person you are making them for. How about Space Boy, Super Star, Super Cool, Disco Star, or Disco Baby?

You will need:

Acetate sheet (available
    from copy stores)
Letter transfers
Silver foil card
Scissors
Double-sided tape
Silver star sequins
Holographic "dotty" card
White glossy card
Ruler
Silver envelope

To make the card:

1 Take the sheet of acetate and rub letter transfers onto it to spell out "Pop Star" or a similar slogan.

2 Cut a piece of silver foil card into a square 2 by 2 in.

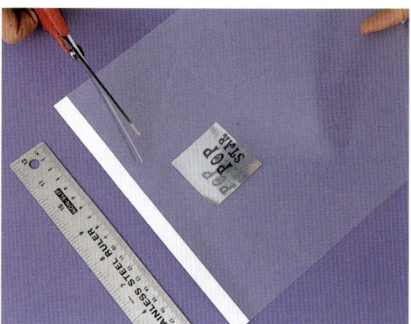

3 Cut a square 2¼ by 2¼ in. from the acetate, making sure that the words are centered. Snip off the corners from the square diagonally.

7 Put tape along the last flap and stick it to the back of the card to seal the sequins in.

8 Cut a square of the holographic card 2¾ by 2¾ in.

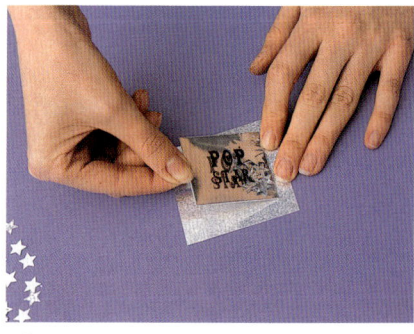

9 Put double-sided tape on the back of the pocket and tape it to the square.

10 (Left) Cut an oblong of white gloss card 9¾ by 5 in. Score it and fold it in half to make a blank card.

11 (Right) Using double-sided tape, attach the square and pocket to the front of the blank and your card is complete. Team the card with a sparkling silver envelope.

4 Using double-sided tape, fix the silver square behind the acetate so that the words are centered. Place a piece of tape along three of the edges, leaving one open.

5 Peel off the backing on the tape and fold the acetate flaps to the back of the silver card to form a pocket.

6 Take a handful of star sequins and slip them inside the pocket.

To make the CD holder:

1 Make a holder for the CD out of the holographic card. It should be slightly larger than a CD with four triangular flaps that fold inward. Draw the fold lines with a ruler. Score along the lines and fold inward over a CD.

2 Make a Pop Star pocket following steps 1 to 7. Stick the pocket to the flaps with tape. To seal the holder add more tape.

Grandparents

"How does your garden grow" plant holder and card.

Whether the recipient has a large garden or a window box, this ivy-themed set will appeal. The plant holder will accommodate two small plant pots and can be lined with waxed paper or plastic to waterproof it.

Here a sheet of store-bought handmade paper has been used, made from cotton rag and embedded with seeds. When you shake the paper the hundreds of tiny seeds stored inside it rattle. It is a tough handmade paper, sturdy enough to support the weight of the plants.

You could try planting scraps of seed paper to see what will grow. Once planted the paper will disintegrate, allowing the seeds to germinate. Use eco-friendly glue and the whole set could be planted.

You will need:
- Pressed ivy leaves
- Cream-colored pulp
- Mesh (metal or fabric)
- Sponge
- Scissors
- Foam
- Piece of plastic to use as a drying board
- Gold paper
- Glue stick
- Card
- Pencil
- Ruler
- Sheet of green seed paper or the like
- Strong glue
- Tissue paper and beeswax candle (to waterproof) or plastic
- Craft stick
- Twine

To press the leaves:

❶ Two weeks before you plan to make this project, you will need to press some small ivy leaves between tissue paper in a hardback book.

● To make the decorative frames and end balls, see the introductory section of this book.

❷ Start by making a cream-colored pulp. See the papermaking section at the front of the book. Use squares of foam 1½ by 1½ in. to cast small paper frames. Cover them with pulp on a drying board, leave them to dry, and remove the foam (see page 16).

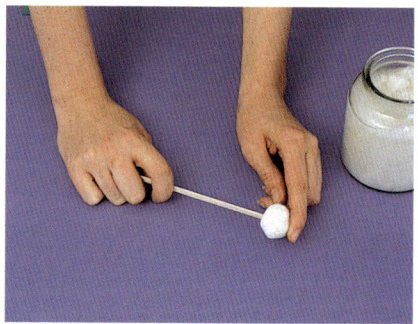

❸ Fashion two balls from the pulp (see page 17). Poke each ball once with a craft stick. Poke the stick in about ¼ in. deep, but do not push the stick all the way through. Leave the balls to dry overnight.

To make the plant holder:

❻ Copy the template from the back of the book onto card. Copy the card template onto the green seed paper. Mark on lines and score them with a thumbnail against a ruler.

❼ Assemble the holder by folding in tabs and gluing it together with strong glue.

❽ Glue the ivy leaf and frame decoration to the front. Line the holder with waxed paper (see page 17) or use plastic instead to make the holder waterproof.

To decorate:

4 Cut a gold paper square slightly smaller than the foam square used in the cast.

5 Paste it into the frame with a glue stick. Glue on a pressed ivy leaf.

9 Make a hole in the curved panel of the plant holder (as directed on the template). Slot the stick through the hole. Push a ball on the end of the stick on the outside. Glue with strong glue to secure it.

10 Wrap twine around the stick to cover it. Work your way along the stick. When it is completely covered, cut the ends of the string and push them through the holes in the plant holder. Roll the ends around your fingers to curl them.

11 Glue on the end ball and your plant holder is ready.

JUST TO SAY . . .

Sometimes you need a little token just to say hello, thanks, or sorry. It could be a memento of times shared with a friend or a mark of appreciation.

Hello

Photo album.

This album is a great place to store favorite photos. You could send it to a friend, with an old photo of you in the front, as a hello.

The kitsch wallpaper covering the album will evoke nostalgic memories of a 1970s childhood. In retrospect, the graphic patterns of the 1970s didn't look too hot when entire rooms were covered in them, but on a small area they look great. This vintage paper was found in a thrift store. You could try flea markets, junk shops, or even your own attic.

You will need:

Card for the cover
Scissors
Two types of wallpaper:
   one patterned, one of a
   single color
Glue stick
4 sheets of yellow
   transparent paper
4 sheets of orange card
Pencil
Ruler
Double hole punch
¼ in. brass screw binders
   (from bookbinding
   suppliers)
Photo corners (optional)

1 Cut two sheets of card for the cover 5¾ by 7¾ in. Cut two sheets of patterned wallpaper 6½ by 8½ in., ¾ in. bigger than the card, to cover. Cut two lining sheets of single colored wallpaper 5¼ by 7¼ in. This is the same size as the leaves of paper to go inside the book.

2 Glue the back of the card and place it in the middle of the wallpaper smoothing out any wrinkles. Glue and fold in two of the edges.

3 Fold in the corners to neaten and glue down the remaining two edges. Press down firmly.

7 Measure marks for the holes on the inside of the cover. Make them the same distance apart as a double hole punch.

8 Turn the hole punch over so that the marks can be seen through the holes at the back of the punch.

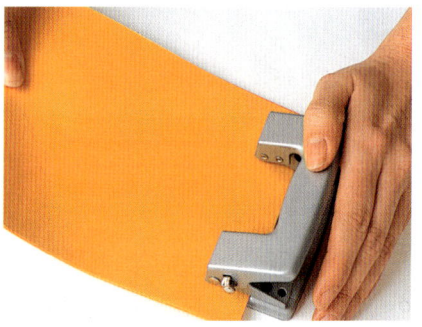

9 Make holes through the leaves of yellow and orange paper.

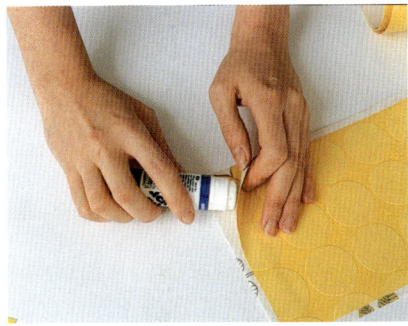

4 Glue and attach the lining sheet to cover the inside.

5 Take the cover and score a fold with a ruler and your thumbnail ¾ in. in to act as a hinge, allowing the front to open. Do the same with the back.

6 Next you will need to cut the leaves of paper to go inside the book. The amount of leaves you can use will depend on the length of the screw binder. To begin, cut sixteen sheets of paper. If your finished album is too thin, you can always cut more sheets to fit. Cut eight pieces of orange card 5¼ by 7¼ in. and eight pieces of transparent yellow. Lay them one on top of the other to show alternate colors.

10 Assemble the book using ¼ in. screw binders. Push them through the holes in the cover and slide on the leaves of paper.

11 Screw down the tops of the screw binders when the album is complete with the desired number of pages.

Variations

Once you have made one album you can make lots of variations, including bigger and smaller ones. Here a small album is bound together with a brass binder on one of the corners. This album is just big enough to house hilarious passport photos.

Thank You

Funky fridge magnets.

This project uses craft punches and brightly colored paper. Craft punches are available in lots of different shapes and sizes and are fun and easy to use. They are inexpensive to buy and take years to wear out.

To cheer up an old refrigerator, use plastic refrigerator magnets that can be filled with anything from handmade paper to newspaper cuttings. For this project, colored paper and a flower craft punch were used. The fridge magnets also make great little presents and can be attached to the front of blank cards to make gift cards. You could use the idea for a thank-you card or as an invitation for coffee or tea.

Assembling the magnets

The fridge magnets come in two halves: a frame and a front panel. The rectangle front panel secures the design when it is pushed inside the frame. The front is a tight fit to make sure the design doesn't fall out. However, there is a little hole in the back of the magnet that you can push a pin into to allow the front to be removed.

You will need:
Scissors
Colored paper and card
Craft punches: small daisy punch, small flower punch, large daisy punch, and a hole punch
Fillable refrigerator magnets
Strong glue

To make a gift card, you will need:
Blank cards and envelopes

To make the card:

1 Start by cutting strips of pale green and yellow paper about ⅞ in. wide.

2 Cut the strips into squares. You will need three of each. They don't have to be evenly cut; if they are a bit uneven the magnet will look more handmade.

3 Punch out orange and bright-pink daisies from the paper.

To make a Kitchen Angel magnet:

1 Using the front of the magnet as a cutting guide, cut a pale-green backing sheet.

2 Cut uneven squares of colored paper. Make sure you can fit three squares across the magnet.

3 Position the squares so that none of the same colors are together.

4 When happy with the combination of squares, add a blob of glue to each to secure them to the backing sheet.

5 Using lettering that you like, print out "Kitchen Angel" onto white paper. Alternatively, you can snip a piece of wording from a magazine or write your own slogan on a scrap of paper.

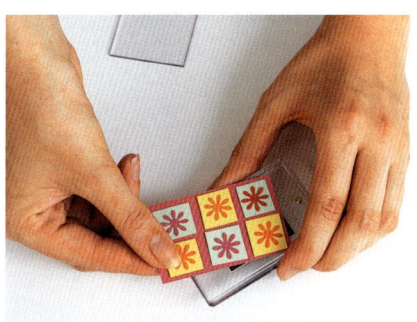

④ Cut a backing sheet from pink card using the front of the magnet as a cutting guide.

⑤ Glue the punched-out daisies on top of the squares and glue the square onto the backing sheet.

⑥ Once you are happy with your design, put it inside the magnet and secure it by pushing down the front panel.

To make other magnets:

❶ Using the front of the magnet as a cutting guide, cut strips of colored card and paper of varying widths but the same length. Punch out flower shapes too.

❷ Put the pieces inside the magnet and play with them until you have made a pleasing arrangement.

❸ Then add a little dab of glue to each of the stripes to secure them before closing the front of the magnet.

Gift cards:

To make the gift cards you can glue a magnet on a blank card or, to make it easier to remove, use four sticky fixer pads. Because the magnets are quite heavy, you will have to glue two blank cards together to support the weight, especially if you want the card to stand up. Contrasting colors were used here and glued together along the spines.

Sorry

Raindrops on petals.

A handmade card might be just the right way to say "sorry."

Make your own paper for the blank card; the deckled edge will look delicately handcrafted. Decorate the card with ink dots representing drops of rain or fallen tears. Splash them on while the paper is still drying.

In this project turquoise ink is used, as it's a deliciously warm shade of blue. Turquoise combined with white creates a vibrant look and a touch of red or burgundy in the form of pressed flowers heats the color scheme up just enough.

You will need:

Turquoise ink
Dropper bottle (available from most
  drugstores)
Spare sheet of paper
A sheet of handmade white paper
  (see the papermaking section at
  beginning of book) or wet a piece
  of watercolor paper
Ruler
Magazine
Glue stick
Pressed flower
White tissue paper

To make the card:

1 Mix one part turquoise ink with one part water in a dropper bottle.

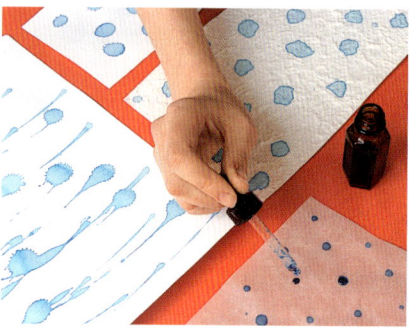

2 Practice on a spare sheet of paper dropping the diluted ink from high and low distances. Low drops will create small, dark blobs.

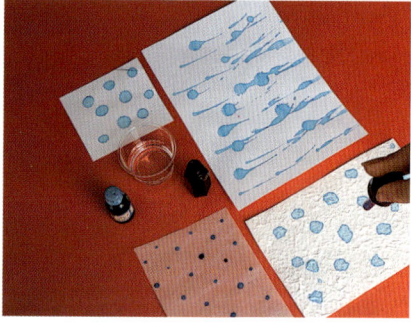

3 A high distance will create a splattered effect and larger, blurry dots.

4 Make a sheet of white paper from recycled paper stock. (Refer back to "Papermaking.") While the paper is still wet on the drying board, drop ink onto it.

5 Keep dropping diluted ink until the paper is covered.

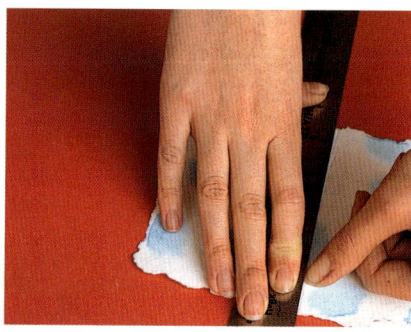

6 Allow to dry overnight. Score with a ruler and your thumbnail and fold.

7 Tear out lettering from magazines. Rip out single letters to spell "sorry."

8 Using a glue stick, attach each letter onto the card.

9 Finish with a pressed flower.

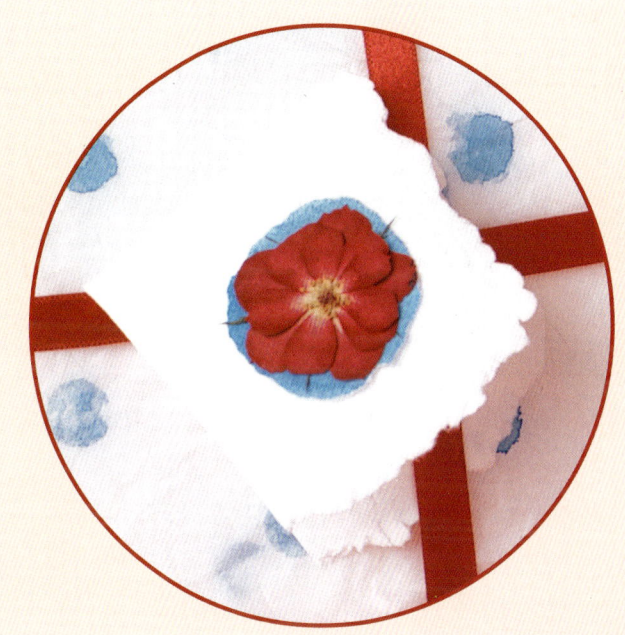

To make the tag:

1 Paint a large turquoise dot on a sheet of smooth, white paper.

2 When dry, tear around it in a circular motion.

3 Glue onto a tag made from hand-made paper 2¼ in. by 5 in., scored and folded in half.

4 Glue a pressed flower in the center of the turquoise dot.

To make quick wrapping paper:

1 Crumple up two sheets of white tissue paper and flatten them back out. The crumpling will produce bleeding.

2 Using the cork from the top of the ink bottle, press ink dots onto the tissue. Repeat until you have covered the whole sheet of tissue. Allow to dry overnight and it's ready to wrap up a present.

HOLIDAYS

This section will provide inspirational and unique ideas for you to celebrate each of five festive occasions: Valentine's Day, Halloween, Easter, winter holidays, and Mother's Day. You will need to check your calendar for Easter, as it changes each year, but it is always on a Sunday, as is Mother's Day.

Valentine's Day

Dinner date invitation, place setting, and name holder.

No one can forget that February 14 is Valentine's Day. For your date, why not cook a delicious dinner and invite a special friend over. You can make a place setting, menu, and heart-shaped name holders, as well as an invitation card to send to your beau.

Chubby tracing-paper cherubs, fat red hearts, and gingham stripes are used to create this visual feast. Use the traditional red and white colors associated with the festivity and you can't go wrong. Humble printer paper has been turned into the menu and place setting so it won't matter if there are spills in the course of the evening.

Before you begin, photocopy chubby cherubs from a clip-art book onto sheets of tracing paper.

You will need:

- Red watercolor paint
- Flat-edge brush
- White and red paper
- Glue stick
- Watercolor paper
- Red card
- Tracing paper
- Cherub images (taken from a clip-art book)
- Black pen

For the place setting:

1 Paint gingham stripes horizontally and vertically on white paper using a flat-edge paintbrush and red watercolor paint. Leave to dry.

2 Cut out five fat hearts from red paper. Make them 2 in. in length.

3 Glue the hearts onto the gingham sheet, one in the center and one in each corner.

For the invitation:

5 Paint gingham stripes onto a piece of watercolor paper. Let dry, score down the middle, and fold.

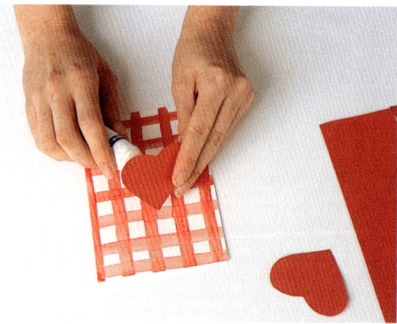

6 Cut out two red hearts and glue one to the back and one to the front.

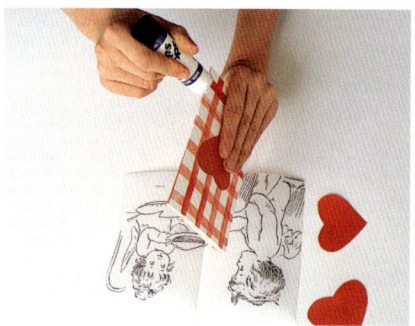

7 Cut preprinted tracing paper to the same size as the card and fold it in half. Run a glue stick along the spine of card.

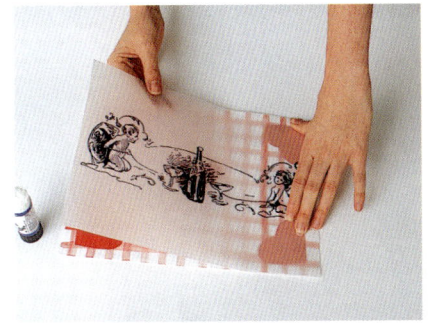

4 Put glue in the corners of the gingham sheet and press down the tracing paper with the cherub image on it.

8 Glue the spine of the card to the fold in the tracing paper. Your card is now ready to send to a special friend as an invitation to a great evening.

For the menu:

Make a piece of red gingham paper by painting on stripes. While it dries, plan a menu of some of your favorite foods. Write the menu on the piece of red gingham paper and wrap it around a wine bottle. Decorate with hand-painted hearts. You could paint them onto scraps of watercolor paper.

To make a name holder:

Cut two fat hearts from red card 2 by 2½ in.

Take one of the hearts and cut a slit from the top to the middle. Take another heart and cut a slit from the bottom of the heart to the middle. Slot the two hearts together and turn upside down.

Cut rectangles of watercolor paper. Paint names onto the rectangles in red and paint a border around the edge. Leave to dry.

Using a black pen, write over the top of the name to accentuate it. Slot the name rectangle into the tips of the two hearts.

Easter

Mini Easter cards with eggs and flowers.

Friends will adore these scrumptious little cards made from handmade papers and felt with seed beads and sequins stitched onto them. They are fun for Easter or great to use as gift tags. Make some pretty papers containing shredded paper, sequins, and glitter to cut into eggs and flowers to adorn the cards. Find some gorgeous ribbons to incorporate and stitch beads onto them to tie around gifts or around eggs.

Steering clear of the ubiquitous yellow, a cool tangerine has been used combined with a hot pink, creating a color scheme that is as fresh as any Easter chick.

You will need:

Sheet of tangerine card
Tube of pink fabric paint
Seed beads in mixed
    colors
Pink felt
Orange sheet of
    handmade paper (see
    Papermaking section)
    made from colored
    recycled paper with
    embedded sequins
    and glitter
Needle and pink or
    yellow thread
Daisy sequins
Glue
Ribbon
Assorted scraps of
    handmade paper

To make the mini "egg" card:

1 Cut the card into a rectangle 3 by 6¼ in. and fold to make a mini blank card.

2 Using the fabric paint, blob paint into each of the corners.

3 Drop a single seed bead onto the blob. You could use four different colored seed beads.

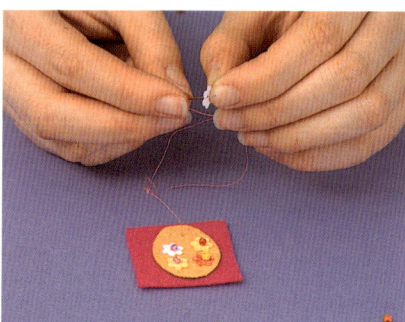

7 Come back through the layers in a different position and sew on another flower sequin and bead. Repeat until you have sewn on five flower sequins and beads. Tie off at the back.

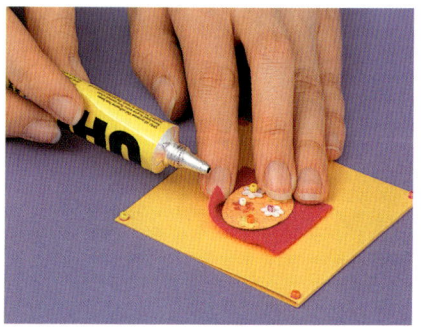

8 Glue the felt and paper egg to the card.

4 Cut a square of felt 1½ by 1½ in.

5 Take a piece of orange handmade paper and draw an egg shape roughly 1¼ in. long. Cut the egg out.

6 Place the egg on the square of felt. Using a small sharp needle, threaded with pink thread, sew through the layers of paper and felt. Thread a daisy sequin followed by a seed bead. Sew back through the layers to secure.

For the other mini cards:

Mini cards can be made in the same way by cutting small flowers and eggs from left-over scraps of paper. Stitch them to felt and glue onto cards 3 by 3 in.

Eggs in a basket tag:

This is made from two pieces of stitched felt sewn up with beads to form a pocket. Stitch a loop of ribbon inside the pocket to form a handle. Decorate the front with a flower cut from white paper stitched with a sequin and bead. Slip in mini eggs cut from assorted scraps of handmade paper.

Mother's Day

Flower photo frame and tinted photo.

Moms are the best friends you can ever have. Reward your mom for her love and friendship with a handmade photo frame. To make this an extra-special gift, you can hand-color a photo too. Before color photography was invented, black-and-white photos were colored by hand with a fine brush. Artists only had a few minutes to apply the color and they had a limited palette of stock colors to work with. Often colors were applied slightly out of place and the colors bore little resemblance to reality. Color a black-and-white photo (or a black-and-white photocopy of a color photo) of you as a child. Make it cute by overdoing the colors, all rosy cheeks and roses.

The frame can either be made by hinging two pieces of mounting board, allowing the frame to stand up like a card, or by hanging it up with a ribbon and a brass ring.

You will need:

- Mounting board
- Pencil
- Knife
- Metal ruler
- Cutting mat
- Pink petal paper
- Glue stick
- Scissors
- Photocopy of an old photo or vintage postcard
- Watercolors and brush
- White school glue
- Pink crepe paper
- Japanese lace paper in purple, pink, and lilac
- Gold "Mother's Day" stickers to put inside the frame
- Gold ring and ribbon, if hanging

1 Decide what size frame you want to make. Here it is 4¾ by 6¼ in. and the window is 2¾ by 3¾ in. Draw the frame and window on a piece of mounting board. Make the window nearer the top by ⅛ in.

2 Cut out the window using a knife and metal ruler on a cutting mat. Start from the corners and cut diagonally, then cut along the edges.

3 Cut two panels the same size, one for the back and one for the inside. The inside needs to be slightly shorter lengthwise.

7 Cut a sheet of petal paper 7¼ by 10 in. Cover with glue and lay on the two panels, leaving a gap. Glue two strips of paper across the gap as a hinge.

8 Fold the edges of the paper over the board and glue them down.

9 Cut a covering sheet 6 by 8¾ in. and glue it to cover the top of the mounting boards.

To make the flower buds:

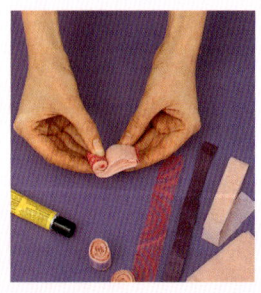

1 To decorate, cut strips of pink crepe paper about 1 in. wide. Cut strips of lilac, purple, and pink Japanese lace papers to the same width but slightly longer. Roll the strips of crepe and lace paper together (with the lace paper on the outside) to form a roll. Glue the end piece of lace paper around the roll. Repeat this as many times as desired. You can cut the rolls in half using strong scissors to create rolls of varying heights.

4 Cover the front frame panel with pink petal paper by rubbing a glue stick over the frame and the paper and pressing together. Cover by folding the top two edges of the pink paper onto the board. Fold in the corners and rub with a glue stick. Press down.

5 Cut the paper that is covering the window diagonally with a knife and ruler. Fold the triangles back in on themselves. The frame on the right shows the finished result.

6 Cut off any extra paper, glue at the back, and press down.

10 Now that everything is covered, you can prepare a picture to frame. Photocopy the image and paint with watercolors and leave to dry.

11 Gloss over the picture with white school glue to seal in the color and to give it a shiny surface. Allow to dry and then cut out.

12 Fold the covered mounting board over and position your photo on the front panel. Run strong glue inside the cover leaving the outer edge free to allow the photo to be altered.

2 Glue the rolls to the front of the frame using strong glue. You can position them in the corners or go crazy and glue them everywhere. You could finish by putting a sticker with the wording "Happy Mother's Day" inside the frame.

Frame to hang up:

To make a frame that you can hang up, repeat steps 1 to 6. For the back of the frame, cover a single piece of board in petal paper. Assemble the frame and photo and decorate as before (steps 1 and 2 at left). Glue a short piece of ribbon and a brass ring to the back with strong glue, leave it to dry, and the frame can be hung up.

Halloween

Halloween cat and witch's hat.

This Halloween cat is sleek and slinky. Newspaper pulp is brushed with a plastic comb to create the look of fur, and silk strands are used to create whiskers. Handmade paper embedded with orange silk strands is used to make the pumpkin card.

Send these spooky cards as invites to a party or an evening of ghost stories. The strong, bright colors associated with Halloween make these cards unforgettable.

An upturned witch's hat (or cone of paper) can be used as a trick-or-treat bag. Stencil gold stars onto it and stuff it full of candies. (If somebody forgets their costume, they can always pocket the candies and wear the hat!)

The black cat could also be used for a good luck card if you change the star stenciled in the background to a four-leaf clover.

You will need:
Handmade paper (made from newspaper)
White paper
Pencil
Black pen
Scissors
Silk strands
Lime-green paper
Black, gold, and white acrylic
Glue
Orange, black, and purple card
Gold studs
Purple sparkle stones

For the pumpkin card you will also need:
Handmade orange paper

For the star stencil you will also need:
Plastic sheet
Knife and cutting mat
Stencil brush

For the witch's hat you will also need:
Bookbinder's pricker or skewer
Black elastic
Candies

To make the cat card:

1 Take the sheet of handmade paper (made from newspaper pulp brushed with a comb). Paint with black acrylic and leave to dry.

2 Make a cat template from a piece of card and place on back of the hand-made paper (gray side). Draw around it with a black pen.

3 Cut out the cat.

4 Glue whiskers made from silk strands to the back of the cat's face.

5 Cut out two green eyes and a collar.

6 With white paint, add a sparkle to the eyes by painting the corners.

7 Glue the cat onto the orange card, then the eyes and collar. Finish with gold studs glued to the collar and purple sparkle stones glued to the centers of the eyes.

To make the pumpkin card:

Stencil gold stars onto purple card. Cut out an oval from handmade orange paper, and decorate with fiendish eyes and a mouth cut from black paper.

To make a star stencil:

1 Draw stars on white paper with a pencil.

2 Put a piece of plastic over the top and trace around it.

3 Cut out the stars with a knife on a cutting board. Start by cutting from the point. Push the star out when you have cut around it.

4 Position the plastic stencil diagonally across an orange card (scored and folded). Use gold acrylic paint and a scrap of plastic as a pallet. Put a little paint on the stencil brush and hold it vertically. Stipple it over the plastic stencil and onto the card. Repeat with the other star. Stencil about six stars onto your card, or more if you prefer.

To make the witch's hat trick-or-treat bag:

Stencil stars onto black card and leave to dry. Roll the card to make a cone shape. When you have made a cone you are happy with, glue the loose edge to the cone.

Turn the cone upside down and place it on a piece of black card. Draw around the top of the cone. Draw a larger circle around this circle to form the brim of the hat. Cut out the larger circle from the card. Using a knife, make slits from the center of the inner circle to the edge to form tabs. Slot the cone inside the brim and glue the tabs inside the cone.

Using a bookbinder's pricker or the point of a skewer, make a hole on either side of the cone just under the brim. Thread black elastic through and knot the ends to form a handle. Line with lime-green paper to cover the tabs and fill with candy.

Winter Holidays

Sparkly snowflakes by Louise McSweeney.

This is a very contemporary card that suits both Christmas and Hanukkah, without a kitschy Rudolph in sight. Sparkling, pearly, frosty snowflakes set the scene for these holiday cards, gift tags, and bags. Icy lilac, cool silver, bright white, and iridescent glitter replace the traditional old strong reds, greens, and blues.

    The snowflake is created from a handmade foam stamp that could also be used to make matching wrapping paper. The only other thing you could possibly need for the holidays is some real snow to complete the shimmering spectacle.

You will need:
- Black pen
- Foam
- Scissors
- Glue stick
- Plastic lid from the top of a jar of candies
- Lilac stamp pad
- White card
- Glitter fabric paint
- Pearlescent lilac card
- A drafting compass or something round
- Knife and cutting mat
- Glue
- Double-sided sticky pads
- Curling ribbon for the tags

1 Draw a snowflake approximately 2¾ in. in length on foam with a black pen.

2 Cut around the snowflake.

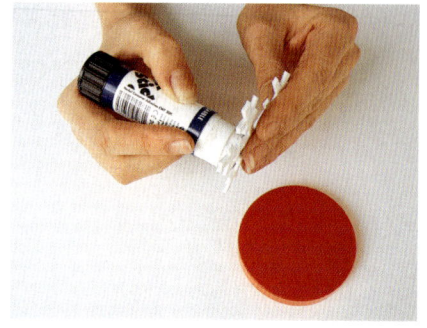

3 Glue the snowflake onto an old plastic lid.

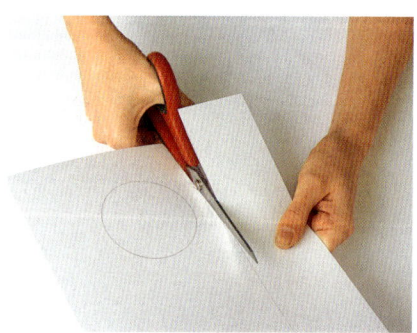

7 Cut a rectangle of lilac card 5½ by 11 in. Score and fold it in half to make a blank card. Inside the blank draw a circle approximately 2⅞ in. in diameter either with a compass or by drawing around something circular.

8 Using a knife and cutting board, cut around the circle by following the line. Work slowly, without taking your blade out of the groove (this will keep the edge from being jagged).

9 Turn the card over and dot blobs of glitter paint around the edge of the circle opening.

To make tags:

Make small blank cards to use as tags and decorate in the same way as steps 3 to 6. Or simply stick a stamped snowflake onto a circle of white card. Thread some curling ribbon through to attach.

4 Cover the snowflake with lilac ink, using an ink pad.

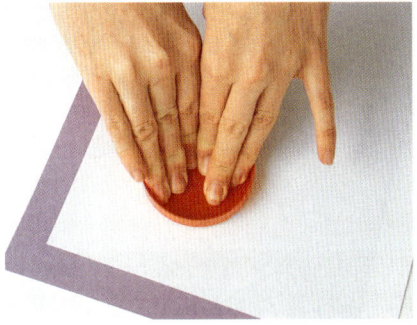

5 Stamp it onto a piece of white card.

6 Go over the snowflake lines with glitter and leave to dry.

10 Cut out the snowflake.

11 Attach double-sided sticky pads to the underside of the snowflake.

12 Stick the snowflake to the empty center of the card, making sure it is centered.

For the bag you will need:

Pearlescent lilac gift bag
White mulberry paper
Snowflake sequins

To decorate the bag:

Decorate the front of the bag with mulberry paper circles, snowflake sequins, and a stamped snowflake.

13 Attach wording written on white card such as "snowflake," or a traditional "Merry Christmas" or "Happy Hanukkah."

Angel Decorations

Twelve winged angels.

As a finale to this book, these twelve winged angels can be used as Christmas decorations or strung on twinkle lights to make unique garlands. Alternatively, give them to friends and relatives as gifts throughout the year.

Each angel is made from materials and techniques shown in previous projects, including: a paw print angel from the Baby project, a gingham angel

from the Valentine's Day project, a striped angel from the Get Well Soon project, and a rubber-stamped angel from the Bon Voyage project. You could also try, for example, handmade paper angels, holographic angels, spotted angels, antiqued angels, pressed flower angels, laced angels, stitched angels, retro wallpaper angels, handmade paper angels, and have lots of heavenly fun making them.

To make an angel you will need:
    Card for template
    Fine black pen and colored pencil crayons
    Gold embroidery thread
    Glue stick
    Scraps of card and embellishing materials from
      the other projects

1. On white paper draw a round head with a fine black pen approximately 1½ in. in diameter. You could copy the faces here or make your own caricatures of friends. Color in with pencil crayons and cut it out.

2. Draw a template of a body onto the reverse side of card. Draw wings on white card or lighter colored card than the body and cut them out.

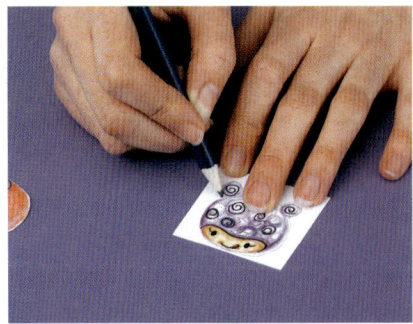

3. Draw around the head on the reverse side of a piece of card so that the head will match the body. Cut it out.

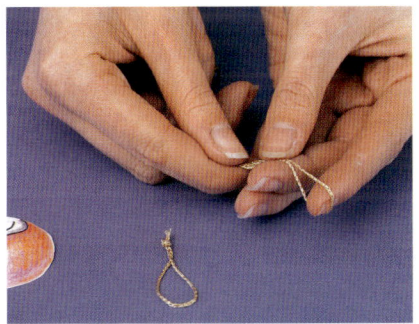

4. Make a loop from gold crochet thread or cord; knot the ends together in a double knot.

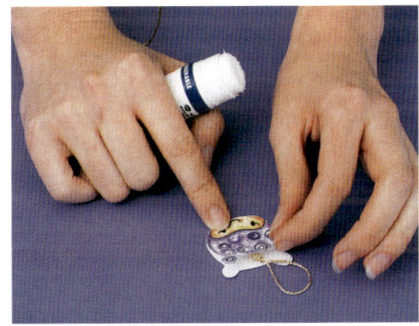

5. Sandwich the ends of the knot in between the paper head and the card back and glue the three together with a glue stick.

6. Collage the head, wings, and body together, overlap them and glue together.

7. Decorate the angel using a previous method from the book. Here a snowflake is used from the Winter Holidays project.

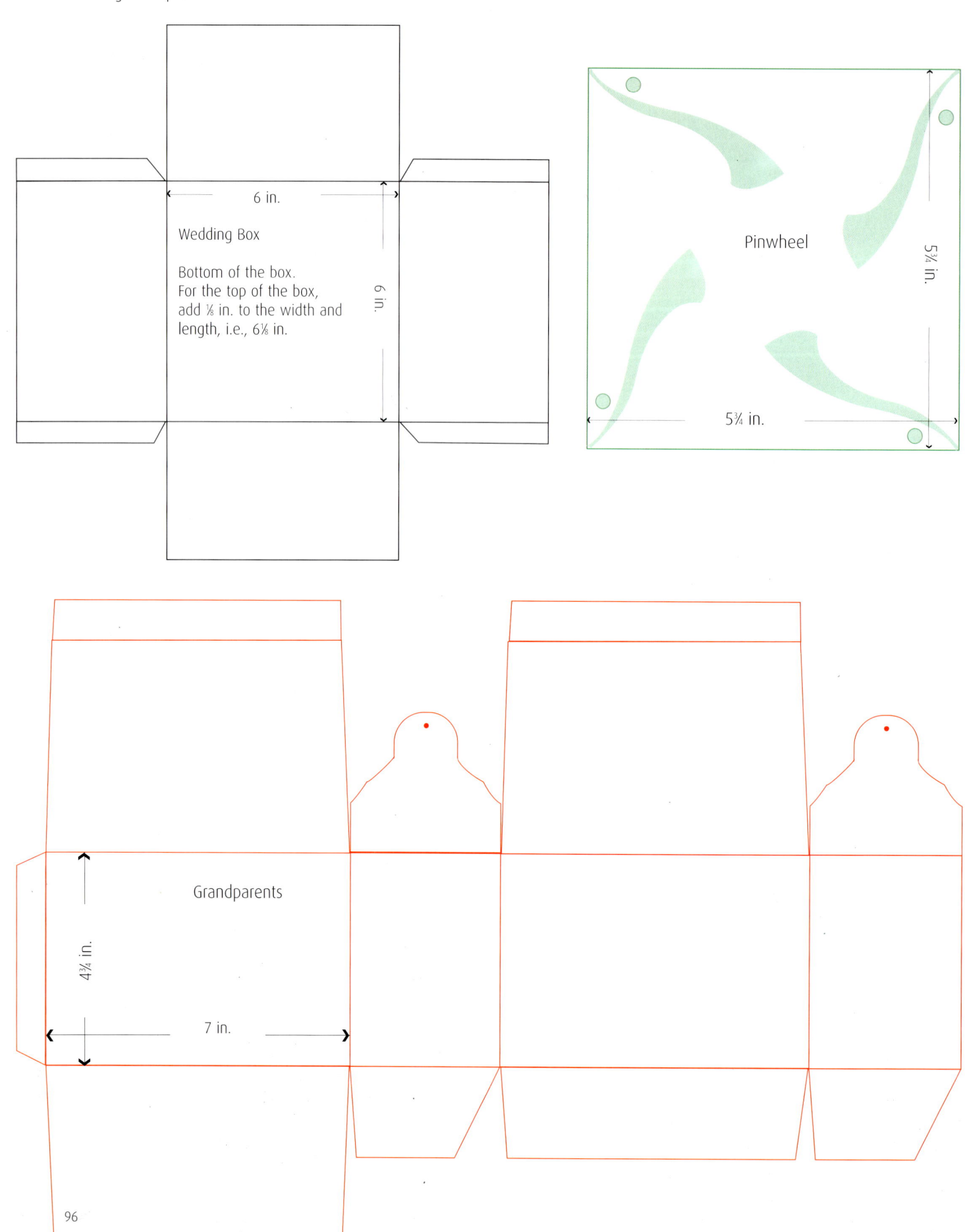

6 in.

6 in.

Wedding Box

Bottom of the box.
For the top of the box,
add ⅛ in. to the width and
length, i.e., 6⅛ in.

Pinwheel

5¾ in.

5¾ in.

Grandparents

4¾ in.

7 in.